Contents

The Good Life

C000174074

The good life

Demos Collection / Issue 14

Editors
Ian Christie & Lindsay Nash

Commissioning Editors
Ian Christie & Perri 6

Editorial Team
Debbie Porter
Tom Hampson
Emma Garman

Layout
Victoria Jones

Cover illustration
Steve Bell

Production Manager
Lindsay Nash

Printed in Great Britain by
Redwood Books, Trowbridge

Demos Collection is
published by Demos:
9 Bridewell Place
London EC4V 6AP

Tel: 0171 353 4479
Fax: 0171 353 4481

mail@demos.co.uk
www.demos.co.uk

ISBN 1 898 309 06 X

Demos is an independent think tank
committed to radical thinking on the
long-term problems facing the UK and
other advanced industrial societies.

Demos gratfully acknowledges
core funding from:
Esmée Fairbairn Charitable Trust,
Joseph Rowntree Charitable Trust,
Cable and Wireless, Northern
Foods, Pearson, Shell International,
BDO Stoy Hayward, National
Westminster Bank, the RAC, the
Inland Revenue Staff Federation, the
Lord Ashdown Charitable Settlement,
Tesco plc and Tedworth Charitable
Trust.

On the good life

Perri 6 and **Ian Christie** make the case for returning the idea of the good life to public debate and policy.

'Life, liberty and the pursuit of happiness' is how the American Declaration of Independence sums up the elements of the good life. The pursuit of happiness is rarely spoken of in public life today. Instead, we talk mainly of economic growth and higher consumption. But the notion that 'growth' is the fundamental aim of public policy, and a proxy measure for progress in quality of life, is now challenged on many fronts. Increasingly, other goals and yardsticks of progress are seen as being just as vital to society, if not more so: buttressing social capital, making a transition to an economy that is environmentally sustainable, creating a more 'inclusive' society. Many of the contributors to this Demos *Collection* consider these ideas and use them to pose a challenge to the prevailing conception of the good life as an individualist project, whose object is the maximisation of personal satisfactions, and whose main yardstick is that of material success – the accumulation of material goods and status. Its ethos is brutally summed up in the message of an American bumper sticker – 'the guy with the most toys when he dies wins'. More subtly, it is embedded in the ways in which our politics has come to express its values and make decisions: the bedrock value is that of economic measurement, and the decision-making procedures are geared to the present, or at best the short-term future bounded by the next election. We are fixated on the procedures through which we generate the resources for the good life, not on its content.

The contributors to this Demos Collection pose a challenge to this inflation of the good life and individualised economic growth. They focus not only on the *means* of pursuing happiness but also on the nature of the *outcomes* we seek individually and collectively. They raise questions, in short, about the possibility of our pursuing the good life, understood as a life that not only brings personal satisfactions but is also decent and ethically lived. It is time to bring the idea of the good life back into the foreground of our public conversation. A sign that this is happening is the burgeoning interest in new forms of social and environmental indicators of progress in achieving desired outcomes and avoiding known ills, and the mounting critique of standard measures of 'progress' in economics, business reporting, and investment.

The avoidance of the nature of the good life in political debate will not be viable in the next century. A number of powerful forces will see to this, and they are explored by the authors in this *Collection*:

- First, the evidence is conclusive that, beyond a certain point of affluence, the achievement of ever higher levels of material well-being and of income does not lead to increased happiness. The consumer society is chasing a rainbow, as Bob Worcester shows in his article; growth, money and what they can buy us is necessary but very far from sufficient for well-being. 'Having it all' is impossible; the attempt can turn, as discussed here by Helen Wilkinson, into addiction and compulsiveness.

- Second, the search for self-fulfilment associated with satiation or disillusionment with the joys of material affluence does not only point us towards modern remedies such as therapy (see Francis Hope's essay) or a better understanding of what psychology can tell us about the sources of happiness, as discussed by Michael Argyle. It also directs us towards a rediscovery of old ideas about the good life – the 'timeless' values explored in this volume by Geoff Mulgan; the satisfactions of relationships of family and friendship, explored respectively the balance amidst the muddle of multi-stranded lives considered by Geraldine Bedell; the idea of ethical education examined by Marianne Talbot; the concept of communities based on ethical lifestyles discussed by Bron Szerzynski; the value of the experience of the old (see the essay by Tessa Harding and Mervyn Kohler); and the ancient virtues discussed by Roger Scruton.

- Third, the pollution accompanying growth as we have known it, and the globalisation of industrial production and consumption, are now acknowledged to generate severe strains on the ecosystems which support our societies and economies along with all other life. The good life as lived by the USA, with its gargantuan appetite for fossil fuels, throwaway packaging, cars and roads, and what Charles Handy in this Collection calls the 'economy of useless things', is simply not exportable to the whole planet. As argued by David Goldblatt in his essay, the stress on the world's climate and resources from a globalisation of the consumerist good life would be unsustainable. But we cannot expect developing countries to shrug their shoulders and resign themselves to relative deprivation: they have an unanswerable moral claim to a greater level of affluence. This means that prevailing patterns of consumption in the rich West must be changed – away from energy and material intensity, and towards a focus on services and intangible goods – as discussed here by Tim Jackson and Nic Marks, Alex MacGillivray and Charles Handy. It also places a new emphasis on the *localisation* of economic life, as argued by Helena Norberg-Hodge and Adrian Henriques.

● The rising awareness of the unsustainability of 'business as usual' consumption in the West inevitably raises the issue of *judgement* about more sustainable forms of the good life. Ethics are inescapably part of the politics of sustainable consumption, and of any conception of an environmentally viable good life, as Simon Zadek and Judy Jones remind us.

● Linked to this is the debate about sustainable well-being. Does my enjoyment of the good life ultimately depend on a reasonable level of equality in society? This argument, associated in particular with Richard Wilkinson, is pursued here by Will Hutton, and with a Christian Socialist dimension by Bob Holman, who calls for a clear remoralisation of policy on income and deprivation.

● The remoralisation of policy debate is also promoted by the realisation that growth and affluence do not solve the multi-layered problems of society – crime, unemployment, violence, discrimination, and the alienation or exclusion of millions of the poor and ill-educated. The problems neither vanish with the achievement of the affluent society, nor do they always respond simply to higher levels of public spending on tackling them. Policy makers, often with deep reluctance, are facing up to the need to engage in debate about such slippery and passionately contested issues as the best ways to raise children who are able to thrive; what to do about stubbornly anti-social residents in deprived estates; how to educate children for effective citizenship and decent behaviour in adult life; and so on. Tackling social policy problems cannot simply be about 'non-judgemental' measures and debate about inputs and outputs of resources. It must also be about good outcomes, and the prevention of ills; and these are bound up with arguments over what counts as 'good'.

● Finally, our conceptions of the good life in the future are deeply influenced by technological change and the restructuring of organisations as information technology and globalised competition develop. The claimed benefits for quality of life from IT advances and from the explosion of knowledge about human genetics and the manipulation of genes will be accompanied by new risks and threats to the good life. Neil Barrett and Perri 6 focus on the implications for privacy in an age of massive personal data flows and new techniques for tracking them; Caroline Daniel looks at the issues thrown up by genetic engineering for our ideas of quality of life and the acceptability of the pursuit of genetic 'happiness'; and Charles Handy points to the limits of organisational and market trends as we have known them in the era of deregulation and delayering of companies.

In sum, the fundamental questions about the good life raised by the earliest philosophers. How should we live? How do we balance individual desires against broader claims of collective well-being? In the rest of this introduction we try to clarify the main elements in a modern conception of the good life, and consider what these imply for public policy.

Who's against the good life?

It used to be fashionable to say that there are as many ideas about what the good life is as there are people. At current reckoning, that's nearly six billion and rising. But just as humans are 'groupish', so ideas of the good life hunt in packs. So, if some anthropologists are to be believed, there are as many ideas of the good life as there are cultures and sub-cultures. Alternatively, there are evolutionary psychologists who reckon that all our ideas about the good life boil down to a basic few ideas and drives that our ancestors developed in the old stone age.

If you take the first view – as many ideas as folk – then it quickly becomes natural to argue that society, the state, organisations and other people should, as far as possible, get out of the way of each of us pursuing our own good life. It isn't a policy maker's job to maximise happiness: that's for you and me. Rather, society should maximise liberty. On the second view – as many ideas as cultures – communities should decide without interference from other communities how to pursue their good life, but have the right to enforce their peculiar practices on their members, unless they leave for some other community. On the third view – that one basic good life is 'hardwired' in human nature – society might be thought entitled to give the one correct answer a helping hand, even at the expense of liberty, or community cohesion.

If that were all, it would be bad enough. Unfortunately, there are still less cheery views. A common one is that pursuing the good life is almost completely futile. Economist Andrew Oswald has shown that for all the huge improvements in material well-being, economic security, personal wealth and general standard of living, in almost every western country, people are no happier, when we ask them how happy they are, than their predecessors fifty or sixty years ago reported themselves.[1] Moreover, happiness is more or less constant for individual over the course of their lives. As Bob Worcester also emphasises in this Collection, whatever makes us happy, it is more than money.

The late economist Fred Hirsch pointed out twenty years ago that many of the things we want are only valuable because other people don't have them.[2] Power, homes by the Pacific or on the Thames and social status only have meaning because only a few of us can really enjoy them. The more people own and drive cars, the more free access to the open road is emptied of value.

Finally, from the earliest times, prophets have thundered that pursuing the good life is positively wicked. When we're unsuccessful, we have wasted time and energy that could have go on more moral living, and when we do achieve the good life, it's either at the expense of those we have exploited, of our own moral development, of the environment and so on. Either we become bovine by grazing on the pleasures of food, drink, drugs, sex, sea and sand, or we become vilely over-refined and snobbish in our enjoyment of literature and the arts, fine wines and arcane ideas, or we become corrupted by the power or status over others that is involved.

Having learned this dismal lesson, it's hardly surprising that many people think we should give up on 'the good life' and pursue something else – such as liberty, wealth or prosperity, or education, or sustain-

1 Oswald AJ, 1994, 'Happiness and economic performance', Centre for Economic Performance, London School of Economics.
2 Hirsch F, 1977, *The Social Limits to Growth*, Routledge, London.

ability, or rights or responsibilities. Thus, governments do not offer to make efforts for the pursuit of our common happiness. Nor do most businesses write themselves mission statements about creating happiness. Nor would promoting happiness be sufficient grounds for charitable status.

This is not only regrettable, it is unviable. Far from giving up on it, in our view, the idea of the good life ought to be central to what organisations are for. This will take some defending against the various advocates of individualism, communitarianism, biological determinism, futility, jeopardy and wickedness. But the effort is worth making. As Geoff Mulgan argues in this *Collection*, politics cannot be based simply on process, confined to managing the procedures underpinning economic development: we cannot escape facing up to the great questions of ethics about the *content* of our lives and the *outcomes* of our strivings.

The fact is that most of the things that big organisations end up being for are not really very valuable for their own sake. At best, like economic security, they are conditions in which the good life can be pursued, and at worst, like economic growth, largely irrelevant and distracting from the business of improving the quality of life.

What are good lives?

For all the cultural and individual variety in ideas of the good life, there cannot be indefinite variety, only plurality. It is an idea closely related to that of a high quality of life. There is a variety of ways of measuring quality of life but if the term 'the good life' has any meaning at all, there are things no reasonable person could count as a conception of the good life.[3]

There have to be very special reasons – such as monastic retreat, or a chosen solidarity with the poor (as in the case of Bob Holman, who writes in this *Collection*) – before we can count a voluntary choice to live in poverty as reflecting a good life. No reasonable person could count a life of mental illness as a good life. Likewise, we cannot count as a good life, one dominated by the persistent cruelty upon, contempt for, and subjection to indignity of other people. In that sense, no reasonable person can speak of a good life being lived as a dedicated racist thug. There are limits to the range of plurality in the good life.[4]

In general, societies have distinguished among good lives between those that are characterised by the satisfaction of basic needs, the sat-

3 Wilson JQ, 1993, *The Moral Sense,* Free Press, New York; Kekes J, 1993, *The Morality of Pluralism,* Princeton University Press, Princeton, New Jersey.
4 For a pluralistic account in the Aristotelian tradition, on which the present account draws at several points, see Kekes J, 1995, *Moral Wisdom and Good Lives,* Cornell University Press, Ithaca, New York. esp. ch1-2.

isfaction of wishes and desires, fulfilment of one's most important purposes and projects, and a life that exhibits social meaning. Without the satisfaction of the most basic needs for survival – or at least the means of securing these – only minorities of mendicant hermits can hope to live good lives of the more sophisticated kinds.[5] The term 'basic needs' is used to exclude all positional goods.[6] Of course, even basic survival needs vary between persons, but not infinitely.[7]

A hedonistic life of the satisfaction of one's wishes is something most of us desire sometimes, however casually. We persuade ourselves that a life in the sunshine of California, comprising mostly play, interrupted by the consumption of exotic goods, as depicted in television advertisements, would be a good life. On any wet Wednesday evening in a British winter, this can only seem attractive.

In practice, rather few people aspire only to a life of satisfaction of desires, and many of those who try it, soon tire of it. A life, like that of HG Wells' Eloi, without problems to solve, complicated emotional relationships to develop and make work, is as unattractive as the Molochs' life of ceaseless toil.[8] Even the pleasures of coarse hedonism are impoverished, for they do not engage that combination of concentration upon a valued goal, striving and fulfilment that is often the source of our deepest satisfactions.[9] The achievement of truly satisfying success depends to a large degree on there being a possibility of failure. Satisfaction of wishes is too bovine a life to detain many of us for long.

A fulfilled life is one that has, in modern parlance, some 'project' or, as the ancient Greeks put it, a goal or end.[10] But not anything counts as a life project of a kind whose achievement brings real fulfilment. Few would dispute that a life dedicated to a decent and inspiring political cause, or the achievement of a major breakthrough in the arts, sciences or intellectual life, or a life devoted to the steady incremental improvement of one's skill in any craft, or to the cultivation of genuinely great friendships or to a single great love, could be a fulfilled life. On the other hand, there are tasks so unchallenging, dull, or perhaps even corrupting, that a life devoted to them could hardly be called fulfilled.

There is also a distinct category of good life where the fulfilment encompasses more than the individual whose life is under consideration. In such lives, the nature of their impact upon their society is the measure of their achievement, rather than their own sense of their life's

5 For a popular but more extensive theory of basic human needs than is used here, see Doyal L and Gough I, 1991, *A Theory of Human Need*, Macmillan, Basingstoke.

6 For a discussion of how to make operational the concept of basic needs without including positional goods, and a comparison with capability based approaches that may include some positional goods, see Stewart F, 1996, 'Basic needs' in Offer A, ed, 1996, *In Pursuit of the Quality of Life*, Oxford University Press, Oxford.

7 For one way of dealing with this problem, see Griffin J, 1986, *Well-being: Its meaning, measurement and moral importance*, Oxford University Press, Oxford, 51-3.

8 Wells, HG, 1927 [1894], 'The time machine' in Wells HG, 1927, *Selected Short Stories*, Penguin, Harmondsworth.

9 In Mihaly Czikszentmihaly's terms, 'flow': Czikszentmihaly M, 1995, *Flow*, HarperCollins, New York.

10 Aristotle, 1980, *The Nicomachean ethics*, tr. Ross D, revised by Ackrill J and Urmson JO, Oxford University Press, Oxford. Annas J, 1993, *The morality of happiness*, Oxford University Press, Oxford. See also

meaning. Here, we are not speaking of those who have sacrificed their lives for the benefit of others; of such people, it would be insulting and demeaning to their saintly act to call their lives 'good'. Rather, there are people whose *own* fulfilment is not relevant to the value they or others can attach to their lives. The meaning of their lives is essentially social and benign.

Finally, there are those who make major sacrifices of some of what would make their own lives good – perhaps of the satisfactions of their own needs, or their desires and do so in favour of a project or activity that goes beyond the ordinary call of duty. The measure of the sacrifice is so great that we classify the calibre of their lives by the significance of their lives for others and for posterity.

In this way, the dreary conventional dichotomy between two meanings of the good life, between the pursuit of self-interested satisfaction, however enlightened, and the commitments of altruism and the 'ethical life', needs to be re-cast. Above the level of the satisfaction of basic needs, any reasonable conception of the good life involves *both*.

At the very least, then, the demands of virtue place some constraints upon any idea of the good life, and the reasonable conceptions of human aspirations set some limits to what duty can reasonably demand of us: the point about saints is that they do not confine their virtue to that which is merely their duty. Of course, self-interest and morality often conflict, and this cannot be explained away. But they do not form two wholly independent, complete accounts of the good life.[11]

Social arrangements for promoting good lives

Although privacy, occasional solitude and retreat are part of any good life, none of these tiers in the hierarchy of types of good life are turned inward upon the self. But more than this, all involve people in acting on their 'nosy' preferences about how others should live. Even lotus eaters need communities of friends, and when they have children, they begin to have preferences about how other parents bring up their children who will play with and grow up with their own.

This means that the simple idea is unworkable, that society should be so arranged that it should just leave individuals to pursue the good life as they see it. There are good and bad 'nosy' preferences, and society needs some way to filter them. On the other hand, unfettered paternalism, whereby society would impose upon people a state-backed conception of the good life, would do violence to many people's own con-

Singer, P, 1994, *How Are We to Live? Ethics in an age of self-interest*, Mandarin, London

11 Griffin, 1986 (see note 7) at page 68 puts the point well: 'Generally, the more mature one's prudential values are, the more important among them is living morally.' For a re-statement of the ancient Greek settlements between virtue and prudence in an account of the good life as one in which central life projects are fulfilled, on which this account draws, see Annas J, 1993, *The Morality of Happiness*, Oxford University Press, Oxford.

ceptions, even part from the independent evil of violating their liberty. This model of top-down *diktat* of the good life has been tested to destruction, accompanied by scores of millions of deaths, by totalitarian regimes in the last century.

How, then, can principles be found for social arrangements that would promote the good life, recognising the plurality of ideas of the good life, the preference for minimising violations of liberty and keeping paternalism within acceptable bounds? We can begin with the question of how far governments and societies can be said to have duties to do things that will promote the capacity of individuals to pursue the good life.

Most people accept that a reasonable measure of liberty and autonomy is the necessary baseline for being able to pursue one's own conception of the good life, and for the cultivation of virtues. Over time, the liberty and autonomy of citizens has developed, and become balanced with obligations,[12] to support other aspects of the good life. However, there are core liberties that cannot, in any reasonable idea of the good life, casually traded off, including a broad measure of freedom of speech,[13] movement, due process and so on.

Clearly, there are some fundamentally important things that individuals cannot easily do for themselves, but which only states can deliver, and that underpin any reasonable conception of the god life. Securing peace is surely the most basic, and, given that the state originated as a means for financing war,[14] one of the most difficult. Individual efforts are usually too puny to prevent or minimise the impact of the great waves of inflation that wash over societies, leaving behind poverty and vulnerability to sickness, and turning culture inwards toward irrationalism, cynicism and despair. The complex variety of its causes are so large that only organisations with the size, powers and resources of states can hope effectively to tackle those causes or even mitigate the effects.[15]

In a society in which paid work (whatever one thinks of the merits of unpaid work) has become central to the way in which many people form projects for their lives, it is not surprising that unemployment is one of the great sources of lack of fulfilment, loss of self-respect, illness and suicide.[16] Therefore, those things that governments can do, not simply to expand employment opportunities and satisfactions for those already in work, but to expand opportunities for those out of work, must be priorities.[17] Even the so-called 'natural' or 'non-inflating

12 Janoski T, 1998, *Citizenship and civil society: a framework of rights and obligations in liberal, traditional and social democratic regimes*, Cambridge University Press, Cambridge.

13 But not absolute freedom of speech: fraud, libel, malice, incitement to racial hatred, violation of privacy can all be reasons for abridging freedom of speech, but never lightly: see e.g. 6 P and Randon A, 1995, *Liberty, charity and politics: non-profit law and freedom of speech*, Dartmouth, Aldershot, and 6 P, 1998, *The future of privacy, volume 1: private life and public policy*, Demos, London.

14 Tilly C, 1992, *Coercion, capital and European states*, AD 990-1992, Blackwell, Oxford.

15 On the causes and large-scale historical effects of the great cycles of inflation over centuries, see Fischer DH, 1996, *The great wave: price-revolutions and the rhythm of history*, Oxford University Press, New York.

16 See Argyle M, in this volume.

17 Oswald AJ, 1994, 'Happiness and economic performance', Centre for Economic Performance, London School of Economics.

accelerating' rate of unemployment can be reduced by government action at the micro-economic level to enable people to enhance their human capital and social capital.[18] Once again, it is clear that many European governments are failing this test.

Most people now accept that it is not too great a violation of liberty for everyone to be taxed at a level sufficient to protect people from falling, through no fault of their own, into a condition where they cannot meet their basic needs for long periods. The general humanitarian principle is widely accepted in mainstream political cultures that, even at the cost of some liberty to the better-off, some protection should be provided collectively against the loss of the basic satisfaction of needs, however temporary or conditional that support should be upon merit, effort or contribution for at least some categories of people.

The criminal and civil law set some outer bounds upon the damage that may be done to others in the course of our pursuit of our own pleasures: noisy parties can constitute an actionable nuisance at law. Social sanctions ensure that one exercises some of the ordinary virtues.

There are strong arguments that society should make some collective efforts to provide everyone with the basic capacities, through education, with which intelligently to choose, identify, develop and pursue life projects of their own. These arguments turn on the fact that few parents have the time, ability or resources to bring out these capacities in their children. Therefore, it is a reasonable test of any system of education to ask whether everyone who makes the effort of which they are capable in the course of that education, graduates with the capacity to undertake for themselves the things that make for a fulfilled life in the society in which they will live. Sadly, it is clear that many schools in Britain and elsewhere in the developed world are failing their pupils in these regards.

Within certain limits, a measure of paternalism by government may be acceptable as a means of promoting the conditions under which any reasonable idea of the good life will have to be pursued. For example, it can be argued that government may reasonably invest in crime prevention and public health promotion, even if the public tends, without reflection, to demand not very effective curative solutions. This level of paternalism can be justified, provided only that the long term underlying preferences of the public for the outcomes of good health and safety from crime are clear, settled and long-lasting, and that gov-

18 6 P, 1997, *Escaping Poverty: From safety nets to networks of opportunity,* Demos, London.

ernment finds ways to make itself democratically accountable.[19] Again, there are arguments for compulsion in pensions but only to a level of provision below which no one could live a life that could be regarded as good, and below which humanitarian or welfare assistance would have to be triggered: it would not be justified to insist that people take out pensions greater than this, for that would impose a particular conception of the good life.[20]

There is a long-standing debate about how far government may go in promoting certain beliefs, attitudes, aspirations, expectations, perceptions of acceptable risk among citizens in the hope to promoting, not a particular conception of the good life, but the conditions under which any reasonable conception of the good life can be pursued. To some degree, of course, this is unavoidable. In a country with an education system that is either publicly owned or where the content of education is publicly regulated, education will at least implicitly promote certain values and cultures.[21] But governments sometimes want to go further. For example, in the 1980s, Conservative governments sought to promote attitudes to risk, work, saving and investment that comprised an 'enterprise culture'.[22]

It would clearly violate liberty and autonomy if governments used strong tools of public action such as coercive regulation or almost irresistibly powerful incentives to induce citizens to adopt the behaviours that not everyone agrees are essential to the good life. But if there is sufficient majority support for the use of 'weak' tools such as information, persuasion and example to reinforce a certain culture among those who share, it is difficult to argue that democratic governments are morally forbidden to act in this way.

Good lives, risk and public decision-making

If someone's ideas are to count as a reasonable conception of the good life, they must surely include some view about how best to handle some of life's risks. Some risk-bearing activities bring enjoyment and excitement to many people – climbing mountains, driving fast, taking psycho-active drugs, gambling, taking entrepreneurial risks. Other risks bring only insecurity and anxiety to most people, even if exposure is the result of decisions to do things they also enjoy – real possibilities of unemployment or losing one's home.

For most people, there is evidence that the good life consists in some rough balance between the enjoyable *frisson* of the former and pro-

19 6 P, 'Problem-solving government', in Hargreaves I, ed, 1998, *Tomorrow's politics*, Demos, London.
20 Jupp B, 1998, *Reasonable Force: The place of compulsion in securing adequate pensions*, Demos, London.
21 Callan E, 1997, *Creating Citizens: Political education and liberal democracy*, Oxford University Press, Oxford.
22 Heelas P and Morris P, 1992, eds, *The Values of the Enterprise Culture*, Routledge, London.

tection against the latter. If we are 'too' protected against some risks, we start to compensate by taking other risks, not necessarily even consciously. The more armoured are our cars, the less safely we drive. This can show up in moral hazard, too: the more that banks are guaranteed against bankruptcy, the riskier will be their investments. Psychologists of risk perception and behaviour call this 'risk homeostasis'.[23]

Insufficient protection against some of the most severe risks that everyday life exposes us to can lead to anxiety, alienation, discontent and revolt, in the form that led to the rise of the demands for welfare in the twentieth century.[24]

There can be no general answer to the question, where should the balance lie between under- and over-protection against risk? While both under- and over-protection are unviable, it is not clear that any Aristotelian golden mean would be sustainable against all the shocks that befall societies. Therefore, the role of the constitutional foundations on which individual and community pursuit of the good life is pursued is not to specify the level of protection, contrary to standard positions on the neo-liberal centre-right[25] or the welfare statist left.[26] Rather, it is to specify a legitimate and just *process* of democratic decision-making on the level of acceptable risk and acceptable protection to sustain the basis on which citizens in each jurisdiction can pursue the good life, since this is a matter of government power rather than of government duty.

It would be hard to credit as a reasonable conception of the good life at all, an aspiration to live in a community where decision-making on the level of protection against fundamental risks was not transparent, not open to popular influence. While many citizens may be deferential, cynical, fatalistic, marginalised, opportunistic,[27] lazy about public involvement or simply in a historic trough of the cycle in such involvement,[28] no one seriously aspires to be any of these things as part of their conception of the good life.

The duty of government in these areas, then, is to innovate in new forms of openness and participation, to eschew the winner-takes-all politics that comes all too easily to ruling élites. Governing by the democratic virtues is an important part of helping citizens to pursue the good life in those areas where they must make collective decisions.

However, there are risks to which the current generations of citizens can expose their descendants – by bequeathing them large public debts, or by leaving irreversible damage to environmental resources that people with any reasonable conception of the good life will want and

23 Adams J, 1995, *Risk*, UCL Press, London.
24 Marris P, 1996, *The Politics of Uncertainty: Attachment in private and public life*, Routledge, London.
25 Hayek F von, 1973-1982, *Law, Legislation and Liberty: A new statement of the liberal principles of justice and political economy*, Routledge and Kegan Paul, London; Buchanan JM, 1975, *The Limits of Liberty: Between anarchy and leviathan*, University of Chicago Press, Chicago.
26 Goodin RE, 1988, *Reasons for Welfare*, Princeton University Press, Princeton, New Jersey.
27 Janoski T, 1998, *Citizenship and Civil Society: A framework of rights and obligations in liberal, traditional and social democratic regimes*, Cambridge University Press, Cambridge, pp. 95-101.
28 Hirschman AO, 1982, *Shifting Involvements: Private interest and public action*, Blackwell, Oxford: 6 P, 1998, 'A culture of constitutionalism for more participation: what would it look like?', in Campbell ID and Lewis ND, eds, 1998, forthcoming, *Promoting Participation: Law or politics?*, Cavendish, London.

will not be able, in the foreseeable future, to replace. In these areas, there is an argument that government should accept some duty to protect future generations from the fecklessness with which today's citizens pursue their conception of the good life.

Conclusion

If we take the idea of the pursuit of the good life seriously, a great many of our political outlooks – liberal constitutionalism, welfare communitarianism – must be questioned. The lazy relativism that holds there to be an indefinite number of ideas of the good life must be rejected. On the other hand, while there are no doubt biological foundations for our typical aspirations and our moral ideas, they permit extensive variation between cultures and individuals. Neither the extreme moralism that demands that our happiness be subordinated to our virtue, nor the crass hedonism that encourages self-centred consumerism, describe well what we know about the things that people recognise as counting as a conception of the good life. The boundaries of what can conceivably be considered as an idea of good life are broad, but do permit us to rule out the wicked, the environmentally unsustainable, the exploitative, the trivial, the resigned – without expecting that everyone should become saints.

Only individuals, households, families and communities can pursue or live the good life. But it does not follow that society and governments can absolve themselves of responsibility for enabling their citizens to do so. On the contrary, when we take the idea of the good life seriously, the principal purpose of their main duties and powers is to support this ⊙

Perri 6 is Director of Policy and Research at Demos.

Ian Christie is Deputy Director of Demos.

Part 1

The pursuit of happiness

More than money

What makes us happy? **Robert M Worcester** reviews the survey evidence on happiness.

'Happiness is a warm puppy', according to Charles Schultz, creator of Snoopy, the American cartoon character. According to a MORI survey carried out in 1981 and repeated again in 1991 however, the prime consideration of subjective happiness for most people is their state of health. When asked to judge which several factors among a list of ten or so things are 'most important for you personally in determining how happy or unhappy you are in general these days', most people said 'health' (59 per cent), followed by 'family life' (41 per cent) and then 'marriage/partner' (35 per cent) and then 'job/employment of you/your family' (31 per cent). These factors stood well above education received (7 per cent), housing conditions (9 per cent) or even financial condition/money (25 per cent).

One person in four in Britain effectively said that money can indeed buy happiness, or perhaps felt that lack of it brought misery, recalling the immortal words of Charles Dickens's Mr. Micawber:

> 'Annual income twenty pounds, annual expenditure nineteen nineteen six, result happiness. Annual income twenty pounds, annual expenditure twenty pounds ought and six, result misery.'

Statistics from 54 countries around the world do in some degree bear out Micawber's homespun philosophy, according to the World Values Survey, directed by Professor Ronald Inglehart at the University of Michigan. It found a .70 correlation between the subjective response that people are 'very' or 'quite' happy, and the objective measure of

Figure 1. World Values Survey Happiness Index and GDP

'Taking all things together, would you say you are: very happy, quite happy, not very happy or not at all happy?'

No.Nation (%)	Not at all	Not very	Quite	Very	Total	Very/ Quite	Not Very/ NaA	Net	HDI*	GDP ($in 1995)
01 Iceland	0	2	55	42	100	97	3	94	0.942	21,064
02 Sweden	1	4	59	36	100	96	4	91	0.936	19,297
03 Netherlands	1	4	55	40	100	96	4	91	0.941	19,876
04 Denmark	1	4	60	36	100	95	5	91	0.982	21,983
05 Australia	1	4	56	39	100	95	5	90	0.932	19,632
06 Ireland	1	4	53	42	100	95	5	89	0.930	17,590
07 Switzerland	1	5	57	38	100	95	5	89	0.930	24,881
08 Norway	1	5	65	29	100	94	6	88	0.943	22,427
09 Britain	1	6	55	38	100	93	7	87	0.932	19,302
10 Venezuela	1	6	39	55	100	93	7	87	0.860	8,090
11 Belgium	1	6	55	37	100	93	7	86	0.933	21,548
12 Phillipines	1	6	52	40	100	93	7	85	0.677	2,762
13 USA	1	7	53	39	100	92	8	84	0.943	26,997
14 France	1	7	69	23	100	92	8	84	0.946	21,176
15 Finland	1	7	72	20	100	92	8	83	0.942	18,547
16 Austria	1	8	60	30	100	91	9	81	0.933	21,322
17 Canada	2	10	55	32	100	88	12	75	0.960	21,916
18 Poland	2	11	73	14	100	87	13	74	0.851	5,442
19 W Germany	2	12	70	16	100	86	14	72	0.925	20,370
20 Japan	1	13	63	23	100	86	14	72	0.940	21,930
21 Turkey	3	12	46	39	100	86	14	71	0.782	5,516
22 Bangladesh	2	13	67	18	100	85	15	70	0.371	1,382
23 S Korea	2	14	73	11	100	84	16	68	0.894	11,594
24 Spain	1	15	64	20	100	84	16	68	0.935	14,789
25 Italy	3	15	69	13	100	82	18	64	0.922	20,174
26 Uruguay	2	18	59	21	100	80	20	60	0.885	6,854
27 Argentina	3	18	53	27	100	80	20	59	0.888	8,498
28 Brazil	2	18	58	22	100	79	21	59	0.809	5,928
29 Azerbaijan	1	21	67	11	100	78	22	56	0.623	1,463
30 Chile	2	22	46	30	100	76	24	52	0.893	9,930
31 China	2	23	49	25	100	74	26	49	0.650	2,935
32 Mexico	2	24	43	31	100	74	26	48	0.855	6,769
33 Portugal	3	23	61	13	100	74	26	48	0.892	12,674
34 South Africa	6	20	45	29	100	74	26	47	0.717	4,334
35 Dominican Rep.	1	25	41	32	100	74	26	47	0.720	3,923
36 Hungary	5	22	62	11	100	73	27	46	0.857	6,793
37 Nigeria	7	20	28	45	100	73	27	46	0.391	1,270

No.Nation (%)	Not at all	Not very	Quite	Very	Total	Very/ Quite	Not Very/ NaA	Net	HDI*	GDP ($in 1995)
38 Czech	3	25	67	6	100	73	27	45	0.884	9,775
39 Ghana	4	24	45	26	100	72	28	43	0.473	2,032
40 India	4	26	47	23	100	70	30	40	0.451	1,422
41 Slovenia	4	30	55	11	100	66	34	32	0.887	10,549
42 Croatia	5	29	57	8	100	66	34	31	0.759	3,972
43 Georgia	6	31	52	11	100	64	36	27	0.663	1,389
44 Latvia	4	33	60	3	100	63	37	27	0.704	3,273
45 Estonia	6	31	59	4	100	63	37	26	0.758	4,062
46 Romania	5	33	55	6	100	62	38	23	0.767	4,431
47 Armenia	8	36	51	6	100	57	43	14	0.674	2,208
48 Lithuania	4	41	51	4	100	55	45	10	0.750	3,843
49 Slovakia	5	43	48	4	100	52	48	4	0.875	7,320
50 Russia	6	43	44	6	100	51	49	2	0.769	4,531
51 Ukraine	9	43	43	5	100	48	52	-4	0.665	2,361
52 Belarus	8	46	41	5	100	46	54	-8	0.783	4,398
53 Moldova	8	48	40	4	100	44	56	-12	0.610	1,547
54 Bulgaria	12	50	31	7	100	38	62	-24	0.789	4,604
Average	**3**	**18**	**56**	**24**	**100**	**80**	**20**	**59**	**0.772**	**10,605**
Correlation									**0.470**	**0.700**

*HDI Human Development Index, based on UNDP data reported in the Human Development Report 1998 (OUP), based on three indicators: life expectancy at birth, educational attainment and standard of living (real GDP per capita)
Source: World Values Survey
Base: c. 1,000 in each country, 1995-97

'Real GDP per capita' (PPP$), from 1995 data reported in the Human Development Report 1998. This is a significantly higher correlation than that of the HDI (Human Development Index), which the UNDP computes using a combination of real GDP, longevity as expected at birth, and educational attainment as measured by adult literacy and enrolment ratios, which gives a correlation of .47 (see Figure 1).

Money isn't everything certainly, but it's said: 'It's way ahead of anything else'. Or is it? According to another poll carried out by MORI in Britain in 1993, when asked 'Overall in the last week, how have you been feeling? Have you been very happy, fairly happy, neither happy nor unhappy, fairly unhappy or very unhappy?', eight in ten (79 per cent) people reported they had overall been 'happy', 13 per cent reported being 'unhappy' and the rest were neutral. Interestingly, there were no 'don't knows'. Two groups associated with lower incomes, women and over 55s, were more likely to report being happy than men (82 per cent and 88 per cent respectively versus 76 per cent) and eighteen to 34 year olds, 81 per cent of whom reported being happy. And those with higher earning power, the 35 to 44 year old age cohort, were least happy, with one in five reporting being unhappy. More were happy in Wales (90 per cent) than in Scotland (75 per cent), reinforcing the English image of the dour Scot.

Surprisingly, marriage didn't make that much difference: while 79 per cent of those who were married said they were happy, nearly as many people who were single (78 per cent) and separated or divorced (76 per cent) were as well. This finding is in contrast with that of Professor Michael Argyle, emeritus reader in happiness (sic) at Oxford (see his article in this Collection), who reportedly has found that one of the most important guarantees of happiness, especially with men, is marriage. Not according to our findings it isn't. A happy sex life, however, was found to be a strong determinant in achieving an overall state of bliss.

Those who reported that they were 'satisfied' with their own sex life were significantly more likely to say they were happy than those who said they were 'dissatisfied'. While 82 per cent of those who reported they were satisfied with their sex life said they were happy, far fewer (62 per cent) of those unhappy with their sex life said they were happy with life generally, and more than a quarter, 27 per cent, said they were unhappy.

An important indicator of happiness right across the globe is people's perceived social class, which is of course tied to income in most cases. As shown in Figure 2, nearly eight in ten of those who describe themselves as upper class report that they are happy, while just one in five of those who report themselves to be lower class think of themselves as happy. If the average punter is indexed as 100 per cent, 30 per cent more of the toffs report being happy (they would, wouldn't they?) while only a third of those in the lower class are, compared to the average.

Religion makes relatively little difference, except that those who describe themselves as 'very' religious are significantly more likely to also describe themselves are happy than those who are 'not at all' religious (see Figure 3). Again, these findings differ from those of Professor Argyle. He found that attending church plays a big part in someone's state of mind, and those who attend regularly are much happier than

Figure 2. World Values Survey Happiness Index by Social Class

'Taking all things together, would you say you are: very happy, quite happy, not very happy or not at all happy?'

					%				
Social class	Not at all	Not very	Quite	Very	Total	Very/ Quite	Not very/ NaA	Net	Index
Upper	1	9	57	32	100	89	11	79	130%
Upper middle	2	14	57	27	100	84	16	68	112%
Lower middle	2	16	60	22	100	82	18	64	105%
Working	3	22	53	21	100	74	26	48	80%
Lower	9	30	42	19	100	60	40	21	34%
Total	**3**	**17**	**56**	**24**	**100**	**80**	**20**	**61**	**100%**

Source: World Values Survey
Base: c. 1,000 in each country, 1995-97

Figure 3. World Values Survey Happiness Index by Religiousness

'Taking all things together, would you say you are: very happy, quite happy, not very happy or not at all happy?'

					%				
Religious	Not at all	Not very	Quite	Very	Total	Very/ Quite	Not very/ NaA	Net	Index
Very	4	17	47	32	100	79	21	58	105%
Rather	3	20	57	21	100	77	23	55	99%
Not very	2	20	60	18	100	78	22	56	101%
Not at all	3	21	56	19	100	75	25	51	92%
Total	**3**	**19**	**54**	**23**	**100**	**78**	**22**	**55**	**100%**

Source: World Values Survey
Base: c. 1,000 in each country, 1995-97

non-believers. With so few attendees in the British population, even among those who profess belief in God, perhaps he's mixed apples and oranges?

In the survey for our book, *Typically British*, published in 1991, Eric Jacobs and I hoped to identify the secret to happiness. We compared the percentages of the adult population in Britain who said they were 'very happy' with those who said they were 'unhappy' to obtain a 'Happiness Index' and found that people who take part regularly in individual sports, or exercise (22 per cent of the population) were more than a third (+39 per cent) more likely to be happy than the average.

Those six in ten who had eaten wholemeal bread were a third (34 per cent) more likely to be happy, and people who'd eaten high fibre or wholemeal cereal were a quarter (26 per cent) more likely to be happy.

On the down side, smokers (31 per cent of the British) were 21 per cent less likely than the average to include happy people among them, while those who'd had fish-and-chips or a fry-up were also among the least happy people in the land (Figure 4).

Unsurprisingly, those who had taken painkillers (such as aspirin or paracetamol) in the past two days were far less likely to be happy than those who had not. One surprise to me, as would be to Charles Schultz, was that pet owners were only marginally more likely to be happy (by 10 per cent) than non-pet owners.

While attending a football match was not predictive of happiness, nor was going to the cinema, a museum, a library or an art exhibition. However, going to an orchestral concert was, as was attendance at the opera, theatre and pop concerts or visiting a National Trust house or garden.

Looking back, we found people generally less happy in 1991 than in 1981, especially with their marriage or partner, how they used their spare time and their health.

Figure 4. What are happy people doing?

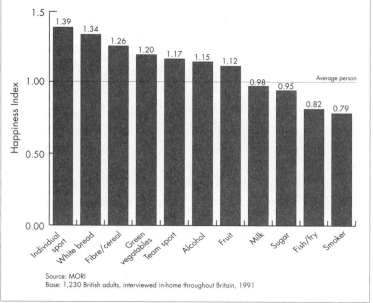

Source: MORI
Base: 1,230 British adults, interviewed in-home throughout Britain, 1991

Joy, gladness, pleasure, satisfaction, enjoyment, delight, felicity, bliss – the American guarantee is the preservation of life and liberty, and the pursuit of happiness, but it was Stendhal who said that 'to describe happiness is to diminish it', and another cynic, Chekhov, believed, or so he said, that 'the more refined one is, the more unhappy'. Perhaps Stendhal should be rephrased: 'To measure happiness is to diminish it'. Some might think so, but as happiness is a subjective state of mind, how else can it be described accurately than by the persons themselves. Are you happy? What would you say today to an interviewer who called on you in your home to probe your views? Today you might be 'up', and tomorrow 'down', but as your mood swings one way, so another person's mood might swing in the reverse direction. The device of the snapshot poll freezes the moment in time, and measures the mood of the nation.

Britain is a happy country, despite its reputation for reserve and stiff upper lip. By the British people's own evaluation of their own happiness they rank ninth in the league table for happiness. But the belief that money does not buy happiness is supported by the statistics that result if you take per capita income into account: Britain ranks only thirty-second of the 54 countries measured, and the Bangladeshi (at least before the awful floods ravaged their country), the Azerbaijani, the Nigerians and the Filipinos are the happiest people on (the measured) earth, when their their low income levels are taken into account.

Factor in educational attainment and health however, and Britain regains its top ranking position, jumping to eleventh in the pecking order of the happiest nations on earth. So what does this prove? That money is by no means everything, and it isn't even in first place ⊙

Robert M Worcester is Chairman of MORI.

© *Robert M Worcester 1998*

Found wanting?

Dr Tim Jackson and **Nic Marks** argue that consumption as we know it is undermining our chances of satisfying non-material needs.

Introduction

What does 'quality of life' mean? What is the 'good life'? Is it related to how much we have to spend? Or to how psychologically and physically secure we are? Or to how 'developed' the society we live in is? In Michael Frayn's novel *A Landing on the Sun*, the title provides him with a metaphor for the task of defining quality of life: the closer you get to the promised land, the brighter it appears to you – *but its brightness burns you up*. Frayn's message is that defining quality of life is impossible.

In spite of this warning, we suggest that society already labours under a particular conception of quality of life, and that this conception is ripe for re-appraisal. We set out an alternative framework for looking at the issue, based on the idea of *satisfying human needs*, and we attempt to forge a critique of the traditional conception using this needs-based approach.[1]

Economic growth revisited

1 This article is based on 'Consumption, Sustainable Welfare and Human Needs' in Jackson T and Marks N, forthcoming (1999), *Ecological Economics*.
2 This compared with 22 per cent in 1977 (a 40 per cent increase in 9 years). See Appendix 1 of James O, 1997, *Britain on the Couch*, Century, London.

Over the past 40 years, personal consumer expenditure in the UK has more than doubled in real terms. This means the average person in Britain has more 'purchasing power' than ever. The traditional economic equation suggests that consumption is a proxy for welfare. The more we consume, the better off we are, and – implicitly – the higher is our quality of life. Increasingly, however, other indicators suggest that welfare and economic growth are not so closely correlated as the traditional equation supposes. Nearly a third of the population suffers from some sort of definable psychological problem.[2] Crime levels, despite progress in some areas, remain high. Resource depletion and environmental degradation threaten the welfare of both current and future generations. Attempts to integrate a variety of environmental and social factors into conventional measures of GDP suggest that the developed countries may now be struggling to preserve 'welfare' despite continued economic growth.[3] Given this discrepancy between conventional economic development and quality of life, there is a clear need for alternative models of quality of life. The model we discuss here is based on an understanding of human needs.

Quality of life and human needs

We propose that one way of investigating quality of life is to consider whether people are able adequately to satisfy their needs. What are people's needs and how can policy makers decide if they are being met?

Perhaps the best-known work on human needs is that of the psychologist Abraham Maslow, who proposed a hierarchy of needs stretching from basic physical needs at the bottom to spiritual needs at the top. Since Maslow's work a number of other writers have addressed the issue, and several important propositions have been made.[4] The model that we wish to use here was the result of a collaborative international project to explore the links between human needs, scale and efficiency in what came to be known as the 'Human Scale Development Project', organised by the Dag Hammarskjöld centre in Sweden and chaired by Manfred Max-Neef, a Chilean environmental economist. The report on the process was written by Max-Neef and his colleagues from CEPAUR (Development Alternatives Centre, Santiago, Chile).[5]

The Human-Scale Development (HSD) project made a critical distinction between *needs* and *satisfiers*, suggesting that needs are finite, few and common to all people, while satisfiers are potentially infinite in variety, and determined by cultural and individual preference. For example we all need to subsist and nutrition is clearly a 'satisfier' for this need, but the choice of which food, the manner of its preparation and indeed the rituals surrounding its consumption vary enormously between cultures and indeed within cultures. The project proposed nine fundamental human needs: subsistence, protection, affection, understanding, participation, identity, idleness, creation and freedom.

The relation between satisfiers and needs is complex. Three general points are worth noting. First, some intended satisfiers are more successful than others, indeed some fail completely. Second, synergies and trade-offs

3 See for example Jackson T, Marks N, Ralls J and Styme S, 1997, *An Index of Sustainable Economic Welfare for the UK: 1950-1996*, Centre for Environmental Strategy / New Economics Foundation, London.
4 See for example Doyal L and Gough I, 1991, *A Theory of Human Need*, Macmillan, London.
5 Published in English as Neef M, Elizalde A and Hopenhayn M, 1991, *Human Scale Development*, Apex Press, London.

characterise the relationship between satisfiers and needs: some satisfiers address many different needs; in practice, some needs are satisfied at the expense of others. Finally, needs should be considered both in terms of deprivations and potentials. The lack of something can be a great motivation, which would seem a more creative understanding of deprivation than offered by the current 'culture of victimhood'[6] so influential in the United States and increasingly elsewhere. Even the example of food as a satisfier of the subsistence need, is not straightforward. Not all foods have the same nutritional value. We do not feed simply to subsist, but also draw other kinds of satisfaction of needs from the process of feeding. As rising obesity and anorexia indicate, our relationship to food is as much psychological as physiological.

Economic goods and needs-satisfaction

The establishment of a needs-based framework for examining quality of life begs the critical question: what is the relationship between this framework and the conventional one? In particular, what is the link between satisfiers and economic goods? In fact, the complexities alluded to above obscure a straightforward comparison of the two paradigms. However, it is clear that if one paradigm is to provide a critique for the other, then it is precisely this relationship between economic goods and needs-satisfaction which we must unravel.

In a recent study[7], we attempted to forge some tentative links between changing patterns of economic consumption over the last forty years, and the satisfaction of particular categories of need. We analysed consumer expenditure for the years 1954 to 1994 and the results can be seen in Figure 1, opposite. [The basis for this analysis is *per capita* consumer expenditure – measured in real 1990 pounds sterling – identified from the UK National Accounts for the period. All figures have been adjusted for inflation, so any changes relate only to actual increases in either quantity or quality of goods.]

The overall increase in consumer spending over the 40 year period is just over 100 per cent. In other words, personal consumption has more than doubled in the four decades. But this increase is shared rather unevenly across consumption categories. The single biggest percentage increase (almost 400 per cent) occurs in the category of recreation and entertainment, closely followed by expenditures on domestic appliances (385 per cent), communication (341 per cent) and travel (293 per cent). The smallest increases are those recorded for books, news-

6 See for example Furedi F, 1997, *Culture of Fear*, Cassell, London, 11. He says that 'our uncertain society has increasingly adapted to its most fragile members... Since everybody is at risk, everybody is a victim'.

7 Jackson and Marks, 1999 (note 1).

Figure 1. Consumer expenditure by category, 1954-94

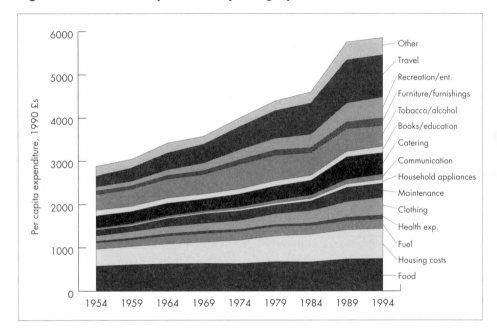

papers and education (14 per cent), and food (29 per cent). The largest increases (in actual monetary terms) have occurred in travel, recreation and entertainment, housing costs, and in clothing.

It is not too surprising that our expenditure on food has not risen dramatically; people's subsistence needs were predominantly met by 1954. However, the need for protection was also largely met at that time, and yet dramatic increases are to be observed in expenditures on clothing. Clearly, clothing expenditure is in part related to the rise of the fashion industry which attempts to satisfy needs such as identity, creation and participation.

The increase in expenditure on travel is not only the largest in actual monetary terms but also one of the most vital (and complex) to unravel from both a needs-satisfaction perspective and an environmental one. By far the most significant percentage increase (about 950 per cent) and absolute increase (around £690 per annum) occurs in the expenditures on car travel. In stark contrast, rail and bus expenditures have fallen over the period.[8] Interestingly, it is possible in this case to correlate these increased expenditures at least partially with increased mobility, measured by passenger-kilometres. In these terms, mobility has increased by around 400 per cent during the period, that is, we travel roughly five times as far in a year as we did 40 years ago.

Of course, mobility *in itself* is not a need, or indeed a direct satisfier. Rather, it operates structurally in the attempted satisfaction of a range of needs, including the needs for subsistence, protection, participation, affection, and freedom. A car also confers status, a suggestion reinforced by the fact that the increase in mobility is less than half the increase in related expenditure: people buy cars not solely for functional reasons.

Does economic growth improve quality of life?

So far we have set out a kind of alternative framework for assessing our quality of life, and formed tentative links between different categories of consumer expenditure and the underlying human needs. We are now in a position to ask whether, using this model, it is possible to assess the effectiveness of increasing personal consumption in improving our quality of life. In other words, how successful is our consumer expenditure in satisfying the underlying needs? Does the dramatic rise in expenditure in recreation and entertainment correspond with an equally dramatic rise in the satisfaction of needs such as participation, identity, creation and so on? Does the rise in expenditure on clothing

Figure 2. Personal consumption: material vs non-material needs, 1954-94

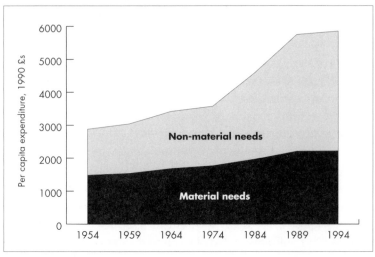

correlate with an increased satisfaction of the associated needs?

Perhaps the first stage in answering this question is to draw a distinction between two different sets of needs. The needs for subsistence and protection can be thought of as 'material needs' as by their very nature they require some minimal level of material throughput to be satisfied. The other seven needs can conversely be considered 'non-material', as they do not, *per se*, require material satisfaction.[9] Indeed, their satisfaction has more to do with processes than with objects.

So when considering how successful the goods and services that people purchase are at satisfying their needs, it is necessary to consider the psychological processes that the goods stimulate within them. For example, if one seeks to satisfy the need for identity through the status symbol of a new purchase then this would seem doomed to fail. As Elgin remarks 'when we equate our identity with that which we consume... we become consumed by our possessions'.[10] In a similar vein it is easy to project our own need to be creative on to objects that we can own, which other people have created – perhaps this is the inevitable conclusion of the 'division of labour', we can only glimpse the possibility of our needs being met through the labour of others.

In fact, there is a growing literature which suggests that we are failing to satisfy our non-material needs, and suffer from alarming poverties of identity, participation, affection and creation. Psychologists are invoking a 'mismatch theory' to account for the symptoms of these poverties: 'compared with 1950, there is an epidemic of irritability and aggression, of depression and paranoia, of obsessions, panics, addictions, compulsions, relationships that are not working, careers that dissatisfy... Advanced capitalism makes money out of the misery and dissatisfaction, as if it were encouraging us to fill the psychic void with material goods'.[11] What is this mismatch? From our perspective, it is the mismatch between economic consumption and the very nature of human needs satisfaction.

Ecological sustainability and human needs satisfaction

Not only is there this mismatch between economic consumption and personal needs-satisfaction, there is also a dangerous gap between economic growth and the ecological balance of our environment. Despite improved technological efficiencies, consumption remains a material-intensive process.[12] The more we spend the more materials we consume, and the more waste we create. Does the HSD model of human needs

8 Air travel has increased massively in percentage terms, although the average absolute increase is moderate by comparison with the increase in car travel expenditure.

offer any insight into this problem?

If we look at the patterns of consumer expenditure purely from the perspective of whether they predominantly address the satisfaction of material or non-material needs, as defined above, then an interesting picture emerges.[13] The greatest part of the growth in consumption over the four decades was related to the attempted satisfaction of non-material needs.

However, this clear predominance of non-material needs satisfaction does not correlate with a reduction in material consumption. Even consumption sectors such as recreation and entertainment, which cater to non-material needs such as idleness and participation, are dominated by expenditures on material goods. What this picture indicates is that we are consuming more and more in our attempt to satisfy needs which are, by their very nature, non-material. This means that our burden on the natural environment is increasing, in spite of the fact that we have long since satisfied our material needs for subsistence and protection. Indeed, the success of these attempts to satisfy non-material needs is highly questionable. As noted earlier, there is an impressive body of opinion suggesting that materialism inhibits rather than promotes the satisfaction of non-material needs. Material consumption runs the risk of reducing rather than improving the quality of our lives.

Conclusions

Two conclusions follow from this analysis – one stark and one hopeful. The stark conclusion is that modern society is seriously adrift in its pursuit of human well-being. For reasons well-known to philosophers for millennia, well-being is not about the accumulation of material possessions. The hopeful conclusion rests in the scope for improvement which this perspective offers. The necessity to reduce our material impact on the ecosystem is normally seen as a threat to our 'standard of living'. However, this analysis suggests that it is *existing patterns of consumption* that compromise our prospects for 'the good life'. Revisioning the way we satisfy our needs is not the bitter pill of eco-fascism; it is the most obvious avenue for renewing genuine human development ⊙

Dr Tim Jackson and Nic Marks are Research Fellows at the Centre for Environmental Strategy, University of Surrey.

9 For an excellent discussion of the problems of the split between these two types of needs see Lederer K, 1980, 'Needs Methodology: The environmental case' in Lederer K, ed, *Needs: A contribution to the current debate* Oelgeschlager, Gunn & Hain, Massachusetts. Sadly the debate seemed to stop in 1980!
10 Elgin D, 1993, *Voluntary Simplicity*, William Morrow, New York.

Sources of satisfaction

Dr Michael Argyle explores what we know about the sources of well-being and happiness.

There is now an immense literature on the causes of happiness. In large surveys, happiness has often been measured by a single item like 'How happy are you?', though in more intensive psychological work we use longer questionnaires such as the Oxford Happiness Inventory, with 29 items and a number of separate factors. These measures have been found to be quite valid in agreeing with ratings made by friends for example.[1] We are still looking for better measures which do not rely on self-reporting. It is possible that happiness may take different forms, for example some people's main joy is religion and others' is TV.

Does money make people happy? We are not quite sure. Surveys show a positive relationship, as in Figure 1 (overleaf), with a levelling off from middle incomes upwards but a strong effect at the lower end. It is not difficult to see why money should have more effect at the bottom of the income scale – it is used to buy food, shoes and other essentials; more money at the top of the income scale is used to buy jewellery, antiques, bigger cars and other things that provide only symbolic satisfactions.[2]

On the other hand, there have been no increases in happiness over time: in the United States since 1946, average after-tax incomes have increased by a factor of four, but there has been no increase in subjective well-being, as shown in Figure 2.

Part of the reason may be that what gives satisfaction is being better off than other people, or than might be expected: Clark and Oswald found that pay satisfaction was higher for those who earned more than would be expected from their occupation, education and so on, but that actual salary had no effect.[3] Other studies show that workers prefer a

1 Argyle M, Martin M and Lu L, 1995, 'Testing for stress and happiness: the role of social and cognitive factors' in Spielberger CD and Sarason IG, eds, *Stress and Emotion*, no 15, 173-187.

2 Furnham A and Argyle M, 1998, *The psychology of money*, Routledge, London.

3 Clark AE and Oswald AJ, 1996, 'Satisfaction and comparison income', *Journal of Public Economics*, no 61, 359-381.

Figure 1. Income and well being for the US

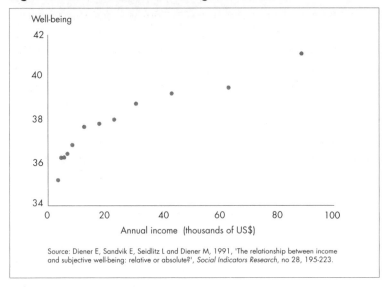

Source: Diener E, Sandvik E, Seidlitz L and Diener M, 1991, 'The relationship between income and subjective well-being: relative or absolute?', *Social Indicators Research*, no 28, 195-223.

Figure 2. Personal income and satisfaction

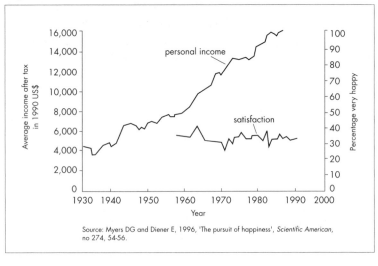

Source: Myers DG and Diener E, 1996, 'The pursuit of happiness', *Scientific American*, no 274, 54-56.

4 Brown RJ, 1978, 'Divided we fall: an analysis of relations between sections of a factory workforce' in Tajfel H, ed, *Differentiation Between Social Groups*, Academic Press, London.

situation where they are paid less, rather than more, if other groups are paid less than they are.[4] Laboratory experiments have found similarly that people can be cheered up by meeting a person who is on kidney dialysis. International comparisons show that on average those in richer countries are happier; however income equality is a stronger predictor, for example, egalitarian Sweden is happier than Brazil.

Happiness and satisfaction are partly due to how we look at things, rather than the material situation itself. We have just seen that social comparisons can work in this way. Another factor is that people can get used to almost anything, even becoming quadriplegic or paraplegic. They also grow accustomed to becoming very rich, for instance by winning the Lottery. This may explain why increasing national income has no effect on satisfaction. In addition, winning large sums of money often has a negative effect through disrupting people's lives – they give up their jobs, move house to an area where they are not accepted and quarrel with their family and friends.[5] And many individuals just look on the bright side, in fact most of us do on average; 86 per cent thought they had above-average jobs in one study.

If money doesn't have much effect in happiness, what does affect it? Social relationships are the most important factor. Love is the greatest source of joy, and people are happier when with their friends. This is partly because of the enjoyable things friends do together, partly because they send each other rewarding non-verbal signals, by smile, touch and tone of voice.[6] Turning to happiness and enduring satisfaction, on average the married are the happiest, the divorced the least happy; those cohabiting, single and widowed fall between.

This has been shown experimentally by studying people before and after marriage and after being widowed. Marriage is also good for mental health: it 'buffers' stress, so if individuals experience stressful life events, a supportive spouse prevents them becoming depressed.[7] Marriage is also good for health: those with marital and other sources of social support live longer. The worst thing about marriage is when is ends: being widowed or divorced is a major source of unhappiness, depression and ill-health.

Figure 3. Marital status and happiness

Percentage saying they are satisfied or very satisfied

	Men	Women
Married	79	81
Living as married	73	75
Single	74	75
Widowed	72	70
Divorced	65	66
Separated	67	57

Source: Inglehart, 1990, Culture shift in advanced industrial society, Princeton University Press, Princeton New Jersey; Eurobarometer Survey (various). n = 163,000

5 See note 2.
6 Argyle M and Lu L, 1990, 'The happiness of extroverts', *Personality and Individual Differences*, no 11, 1011-1017.
7 Brown GW and Harris T, 1978, *Social origins of depression*, Tavistock, London.

Health correlates with happiness; they affect each other especially if subjective measures are used of how well people think they are, or how satisfied they are with their health. This is not the same as objective health as assessed by a doctor and physiological measurements. However, happiness affects objective health too, and subjective health has long-term effects on real health as the positive emotions of happiness affect the immune system.

Job satisfaction is an important source of overall life satisfaction and is one of its causes, though causation is in both directions. Job satisfaction is much greater for those in more interesting and demanding jobs, like scientists, university teachers and lawyers. There are also social satisfactions, from gossip to jokes with co-workers; this is a source of social cohesion and cooperation as well as job satisfaction. As with marriage, social support at work buffers stress and prevents those under stress developing arthritis, heart disease and the rest.[8]

Unemployment is a major source of unhappiness, depression and poor physical health, alcoholism and suicide. This can be alleviated by the adoption of sport or other serious leisure. One such form of leisure is voluntary work, and this has the further benefit of providing people with confidence and skills, which can lead to paid work later.

Leisure is of special interest since it is the source of happiness that is most under voluntary control. It is more important than work as a source of satisfaction for many people. How does it do this? A theory of leisure and work satisfaction was put forward by Csikszentmihalyi, that deep satisfaction or 'flow' is obtained when activities are challenging but can be met with equivalent skills.[9] For example, he found that serious rock climbing was very satisfying. We too have found that serious or committed leisure makes people happy. On the other hand, most of us prefer challenges to be less than the theory implies. Some people seek challenges on their holidays, but the great majority want to relax. The most popular leisure activity is watching TV, which offers no challenges at all. Csikszentmihalyi studied this too and concluded that while watching we are in a state of consciousness 'somewhere between being awake and being asleep'.

Sport can be challenging, but for more people their exercise is non-competitive and non-challenging – swimming, running or aerobics for example – as well as being social. And exercise has a more direct effect on mood by releasing endorphins. We have found that regular sport or exercise has more effect on happiness than most kinds of leisure.[10]

8 Argyle M, 1989, *The Social Psychology of Work*, Penguin, London.
9 Csikszentmihaly M, 1975, *Beyond Boredom and Anxiety*, Jossey-Bass, San Fransisco.
10 Hills P and Argyle M, 1998, 'Positive moods derived from leisure and their relationship to happiness and personality', *Personality and Individual Differences*, no 25, 523-535.
11 Argyle M, 1996, *The social psychology of leisure*, Penguin, London.

Exercise is so good for depression and anxiety that it is now being pre-scribed by doctors. And it has many benefits for health: 30 minutes of exercise a day is sufficient for the maximum benefits.[11]

Most forms of leisure provide social satisfaction, and even TV pro-vides this, by watching with friends or family and by having imaginary friends inside the TV set. We have found that belonging to leisure groups is a great source of joy and satisfaction; the reason is the social interaction and support. For some groups, relations with other members are closer than with other friends.[12]

Religion is a source of happiness that is very important for some. On average, church members are a little happier than others, but the effect is greater on old people. This is partly because church communities give strong social support, but also because the relation with God can func-tion as another social relationship, and because beliefs give optimism in the future. Religion can be good for health too, but you have to join the right religion: Mormons, Seventh Day Adventists and members of other churches with strict rules on drinking, smoking and so on may live four to five years longer. Religion affects physical and mental health in other ways, via social support and 'religious coping' in which people seek a religious solution to their problems.[13]

Are there happy people, and if so who are they? There are consistent individual difference: the same people are found to be happy up to 17 years later. Twin studies have found a moderate genetic factor. And hap-piness correlates with some personality traits which are known to be partly inherited and stable over time.[14] One of these is extroversion, which refers to people who like social activities. Figure 4 shows the strength of this factor.

Why are extroverts so happy? We have found that it is partly because of the enjoyable social activities in which they engage, partly their good social skills, including assertiveness and co-operativeness.[15] On the other hand, neuroticism is a personality dimension that is asso-ciated negatively with happiness.

Figure 4. Cell means for Oxford Happiness Index with respect to high and low levels of extroversion and neuroticism

Extroversion	Neuroticism	
	Low	High
Low	28.1(54)	26.3 (60)
High	40.4 (60)	31.1 (60)

12 See note 11.

13 Beit-Hallahmi B and Argyle M, 1997, *The psychology of religious behaviour, belief and experience*, Routledge, London.

14 Diener E and Lucas R, 1998 (forthcoming), 'Personality and subjec-tive well-being' in Kahneman D, Diener E and Schwarz N, eds, *Understanding Quality of Life: Scientific per-spectives on enjoyment and suffering*, Russell Sage, New York.

15 See note 6.

There are also cognitive factors, that is thinking styles, that affect happiness. One of these is attributional style: depressed people blame themselves when things go wrong, but happy people only ascribe good things to themselves. Happy people have a strong Pollyanna effect: they look on the bright side, for example they are optimistic and only remember good things about the past. There is evidence that depressed people are more accurate and realistic in the way they see the world, but it doesn't do them any good. Having a big gap between aspirations and achievements goes with unhappiness; happy people have a smaller gap between the two. This explains why older people are more satisfied with things: their aspirations have fallen and their achievements have risen.

Could happiness be increased?

Contrary to accepted political assumptions, it seems that increasing income for all has no effect, but increasing it at the lower end of the income scale would. Countries with greater overall equality are happier, which supports the case for moving in that direction.

Unemployment is a major source of unhappiness. It could be reduced by more job sharing, for example shorter hours of work, shorter years of work and so on, but that is a matter for economists. It has been found that the unemployed are happier if they can find satisfying leisure, like sport and voluntary work, and that the latter can increase their employability.

Conversely, job satisfaction is a major source of happiness. There are still a lot of boring, repetitive jobs, although computerisation has abolished many of them. This could be borne in mind when designing new jobs, for example the installation of automated systems. Efforts could also be made to enhance the social satisfactions of work, for example by keeping work groups intact as they do in Japan.

Leisure is important since it is largely under voluntary control and less constrained by material factors, but more could be done to provide leisure facilities of all kinds. Individuals can enhance their leisure satisfaction by leisure counselling, or by psychological techniques for discovering which activities do them most good.

Divorce, which is a great source of unhappiness, could be decreased by provision of and encouragement to engage in marriage counselling, and the opportunity to acquire the social skills for coping better with this difficult relationship.

Not all people can benefit from social relationships and the support they provide, since some are socially isolated. For those with problems, Alcoholics Anonymous and similar mutual help groups are successful. And for those with poor social skills, the greater availability of social skills training would do a lot to help.

Changing people's personalities is possible by various forms of psychotherapy, and four to six sessions can do a lot for happiness. It has been found that belonging to friendly social groups at leisure and work can make people happier, and this is partly because their personality is changed, in the direction of greater extroversion.[16] And we have also seen that exercise is good for depression and anxiety.

There have now been many surveys and other studies of the causes of happiness. Money has little effect, except at the lower end of the income scale. This is partly because people get used to their situation, partly because of other subjective factors such as social comparisons. More important causes of happiness are social relationships like marriage and friends. Interesting and satisfying work and the company of workmates are also important. Leisure has the advantage that it is mainly under voluntary control; benefits for good moods and happiness have been found for sport and exercise, leisure groups of all kinds and church and voluntary work. There are happy people: extroverts tend to be happier, as do those who look on the bright side, whereas those with neuroticism are less so ☉

Dr Michael Argyle is Visiting Professor at the Department of Experimental Psychology, Oxford University, and author of many studies in social psychology.

16 Headey B, Holstrom E and Wearing A, 1984, 'Well-being and ill-being: different dimensions?', *Social Indicators Research*, no 14, 115-139.

Good relations

Satisfying relationships are central to our ideas about happiness. **Penny Mansfield** considers the link between committed relationships and the good life.

Relationships preoccupy us: how to get one, how to keep a good one, how to get out of – or get over – a failed one. These days the good relationship is central to our idea of happiness. We tell researchers that, apart from staying free of serious illness, the quality of our relationships is our biggest single source of happiness.[1] Marriage is one of the most important guarantors of that happiness. Both married men and married women seem to be more contented than unmarried people, including unmarried people who cohabit.[2]

Research which identifies the link between a sense of well-being and relationship status explains why relationships matter. Jessie Bernard's influential book of the mid-seventies, *The Future of Marriage*, identified two marriages; his and hers. She argued that while marriage was good for him, it was bad for her.[3] Research findings from the 1990s show that marriage can produce substantial benefits not only for men but for women too; single and divorced women reported significantly less satisfaction with life than married women.

On average, married people have better health, longer life, more and better sex, greater wealth and better outcomes for their children. Married people engage in less risky behaviour (they smoke less, drink less, have less unsafe sex); while marital breakdown actually induces unhealthy lifestyles for some. The married have more money; economies of scale mean that two can live as cheaply as one or at least less expensively than two. Being better off adds to their health advantage too. With marriage comes a network of help and support; companionship, mutual support, emotionally satisfying 'on-site sex', a con-

1 Argyle M, 1987, *The Psychology of Happiness*. Recent findings from his Oxford Happiness Inventory were reported in the *Daily Mail*, 5 October 1998.
2 Waite L, 1998, 'Trends in men's and women's well-being in marriage', paper given to Smart Marriages conference, Washington DC, July 1998. Using data from the General Social Survey, a repeated cross-sectional survey of about 1500 adults done almost every year between 1972 and 1996, for a total sample of 35,000 people.
3 Bernard J, 1976, *The Future of Marriage*, Harmondsworth, Penguin.

nection to other individuals, social groups and institutions.[4]

Does the good relationship have to be rooted in marriage? Few studies have compared married and cohabiting couples. Most research compares those who are currently married with those who are not – either those who have never married or are no longer married (separated, divorced or widowed). Comparisons are based on average benefits of marriage: some marriages produce substantially higher benefits for spouses and some substantially lower; some marriages produce no benefits at all and even cause harm to the adults and children involved. Referring to the 'average' cohabiting relationship is less appropriate, then, than defining an 'average' marriage, because marriage presumes a common element – commitment; cohabiting relationships involve varying degrees of commitment.

Where comparisons are possible between marriage and cohabitation it seems that marriage has the edge.[5] Several writers have pointed to an essential difference between marriage and cohabitation – cohabitation is a declaration of an existing state of affairs with no implications for future conduct, whereas marriage presumes permanence.[6] That presumption encourages partners to plan for the future; it provides a framework for developing responsibilities and a sense of purpose. The expectation of a long-term, if not life-long, relationship encourages investment – the building of assets, both emotional and economic.

So, marriage contributes to a good life – but how do we know that marriage is the cause? Which comes first? Could it be that the healthiest, happiest people choose marriage? Selectivity plays a part, but the positive effect of marriage on well-being is strong and consistent.[7] That being so, why do fewer people enter into it and why are ever more people trying to get out of it?

The common wisdom is that declining marriage rates and rising divorce rates are a legacy of the liberalisation of attitudes that emerged in the 'Swinging Sixties'. In fact, recent changes in relationship formation have their roots in the demographic transition arising out of social and economic developments of the last century.[8] There has been an emphasis on individualisation identified by most theorists as the key ideational change of the century.[9] An approach to life that rejects traditional institutionalised norms of behaviour, individualisation takes many forms; around the turn of the century it was characterised by an increasing focus on the nuclear family and declining

4 Waite, 1998 (note 2); McAllister F, ed, 1995, *Marital Breakdown and the Health of the Nation*, One plus One, London; Waite L, 1995, 'Does marriage matter?', *Demography*, vol 32, no 4, 483-507.
5 Waite, 1998 (note 2).
6 Eekelaar JM, 1980 in Eekelaar JM and Katz SN, eds, *Marriage and Cohabitation in Contemporary Society*, Butterworths, Toronto.
7 Ross CE, 1995, 'Reconceptualizing marital status as a continuum of social attachment' in *Journal of Marriage and the Family* no 57, 129-40.
8 Lesthaeghe R, 1983, 'A century of demographic and cultural change in Western Europe: an exploration of underlying dimensions', *Population and Development Review*, no 19, 411-435; van de Kaa D, 1987, 'Europe's second demographic transition', *Population Bulletin*, vol 42, no 1, 1-58; Cherlin, 1992, *Marriage, Divorce, Remarriage*, Harvard University Press, Cambridge, Massachusetts.
9 Reynolds J and Mansfield P, 1998, *The Effect of Changing Attitudes to Marriage on its Stability*, a literature review to be published by the Research Secretariat of the Lord Chancellor's Dept.

Church influence. The rate and progress of change varied across Western countries, but between 1880 and 1930 most countries began to experience a decline in fertility, a fall in the age of marriage, an increase in the numbers marrying and the first rise in divorce rates above previously discernible levels. These changes culminated in what some refer to as the 'golden age' of marriage between 1950 and 1970; an era of unprecedented numbers of marriages, notably among the young. Thereafter, the numbers of divorces rose while the number of marriages declined. From the 1960s, individualism emphasised self-development, a concern with achieving individual goals, and equal opportunity.[10]

The social role of marriage changed. It used to play a central part in the sequence of growing up and reaching independence, as the launch-pad for adulthood: the marriage contract consisted of an exclusive package of rights that gave status and meaning to a person's life.[11] The difference between Miss and Mrs was very important, absolutely essential when it came to childbearing. For some it still is, but marriage no longer has the monopoly in providing this rite of passage. Now there are alternatives: staying single; cohabiting either with a view to marriage or as a non-committed sexual relationship; same-sex relationships. Childbearing outside marriage has risen accordingly.

With greater acceptance of diversity and choice in the forms of relationships, we have also revised our view of what constitutes the good relationship. This revision is commonly described as a shift from institution to relationship. Marriage as an institution – a legal contract based on social and economic considerations has, according to this analysis, given way to marriage as a relationship – an emotional bond founded upon intimacy, companionship, sharing and communication.[12] In fact, the modern relationship model retains some important features of the institutional model.[13] But according to the relationship model, the essential purpose of marriage has shifted from a social purpose to a personal one: the self-fulfilment of the two individuals. In the 1990s young men and women embarking on marriage have higher expectations than their parents' generation that marriage will meet their needs for companionship, personality development and emotional security. They (at least women) seek the skills to fulfil these expectations – they buy huge quantities of books to tell them how to communicate better; how to have great sex; how to manage conflict creatively. Books, videos, therapists, learning courses : an industry is

10 Reynolds and Mansfield, 1988, (note 9).

11 Mansfield P and Collard J, *The Beginning of the Rest of Your Life?*, Macmillan, Basingstoke.

12 Morgan D, 1992 'Marriage and society: understanding an era of change' in Lewis J, Clark D and Morgan D, eds, *Whom God has Joined Together*, Routledge, London; Collard J and Mansfield P, 1991, 'The couple: a sociological perspective' in Hooper D and Dryden W, eds, *Couple Therapy*, Open University, Milton Keynes.

13 Economics plays an important part in the processes and negotiations of married life, if not in the initial choice of partner. At any period one can detect both institutional and relational aspects of marriage, and within any period there is likely to be variation according to class, religion, gender and ethnic group. While relational aspects of marriage may be more pronounced when the couple are newly-wed, institutional aspects may come to the fore during child-bearing and child-rearing phases of married life. A more relational form may emerge after the children have left home.

being built on achieving the good – the perfect – relationship.[14]

The very use of the term relationship indicates that the tie between the partners is freely chosen and, consequently, freely abandoned when it no longer achieves its purpose. If the point of staying together is to be happy, then why stay when you are not? And why bother to learn how to communicate better or have better sex unless you actually want the relationship to continue? The basic commitment is essential but it has been overlooked in the scramble for the continuously fulfilling relationship So the central question about relationships and the good life is not: how do we become better at relating? It is: how do we become better at being committed?

Commitment is not just about making a promise when a relationship is good, it is about keeping that promise when the relationship is not so good. In a longitudinal study of marriage, couples were interviewed just after the wedding and again five years later.[15] These interviews provide insights into the art of staying together. There appear to be two interdependent elements of the marriages: the relationship and the partnership.

The partnership is the joint project of the partners, the purpose of staying together. It anchors their relationship and in turn, their relationship – the emotional attachment between them – sustains their partnership. So, at times when their relationship doesn't feel good, the partnership is crucial since it articulates future commitment. And at times of change, when the partners become parents for example, having a good relationship will help the partners to work out how to revise their partnership to accommodate changing circumstances. A relationship without a partnership has no anchor since commitment is entirely in the present. When the feel-good factor has gone there is no point in staying. However, all marriages are partnerships in so far as the partners have made an explicit commitment to each other in the future.

What has changed in recent years is that many couples no longer accept that their partnership is defined by traditional marriage. The partners now define their partnerships, marriage no longer defines the couple. And partnerships come in different forms (determined by the particular purpose). Legal marriage is not essential to the creation of such a partnership, but recognition of the partnership by others, particularly those people who matter to the partners, will be significant in helping the couple to reinforce their commitment to each other. To

14 'Marriage is Back', Newsday, 10 October 1997. Interviews with leading figures in publishing 'The publishing industry is responding to what people want ... the trend was in books that dealt with being on your own. Now it's in making the most of your relationships.'
15 Mansfield and Collard, 1988 (note 11). A sequel, Mansfield P, Collard J and McAllister F, *Couples: Commitment and Change* to be published.

this extent the partnership is social, while the relationship is private. The benefits of the good relationship require time: commitment – the sense of being committed and being the focus of another's commitment – buys that time. By stressing the good relationship we obscure the need for frameworks which relationships need to develop and grow. The desire to be free from constraints has made us forget the paradoxical nature of human relationships: that we may find freedom through choosing to limit, not keep open, our choices.

The commitment-phobic hero of Nick Hornby's very 1990s novel *High Fidelity*, puts it like this: 'See, I've always been afraid of marriage because of, you know, ball and chain, I want my freedom, all that ... I suddenly saw it was the opposite: that if you got married to someone you know you love, you sort yourself out, it frees you up for other things.'[16]

Like semi-hardy plants, relationships are delicate. Traditionally trained up a stake called marriage, by and large, they grew into the same shape. Then came the cry from the romantics: 'Throw away the stake! Let the relationship grow and blossom as it will without being tied back.' But if love is to be enduring it must be responsible love, not a duty but a mutual obligation; every act by one partner has implications for the other. A framework for developing that mutuality is essential. Not everyone wants the traditional structure of marriage but we do need some structure for our relationships to hold on to if they are to develop. Instead of a single stake, what is needed is something more like trelliswork, a structure that offers different patterns for different relationships to discover their own routes towards goals they have chosen. Governments want people (especially children) to have all the benefits of marriage but know they cannot force adults into its traditional structure.[17] The state's role is therefore to enable men and women to define and validate new patterns of partnership. Call them marriages or not, these new forms of partnership need to be recognised and supported by appropriate policy and legislation ⊙

Penny Mansfield is Director of One Plus One, which undertakes research on marriage and partnership.

16 Hornby N, 1995, *High Fidelity*, Victor Gollanz, London.
17 See recent attempts to introduce civil solidarity pacts (PACS) in French parliament – allowing couples who had cohabited for three years to enter legal agreements short of marriage. In the UK, the government has published (November 1998) a consultation document on the family, *Supporting Families*, which includes a a variety of proposals to strengthen marriage.

Culture on the couch

Francis Hope

Psychotherapy, as a process that attempts to realise human well-being, must be understood in terms of the cultural context in which it takes place. Where once well-being was to be attained through the overthrow of oppressive sexual and social mores – the bourgeois sensibility of Freud's Vienna – people now seek solutions to an almost opposite range of problems; not those caused by a world that is too closed, determined and bound by predictable convention but one which is too loose, fast changing and fragmentary.

Just how well psychotherapy can help people cope is hard to answer. There is no longer a psychoanalytic monolith. Rather, just like society, it has split into myriad forms, creating both choice and confusion for people seeking therapy (and, arguably, worrying variances in standards). In terms of context, however, one key factor can be identified: the continued breakdown of established social networks and modes of relation at work and in local communities. This has brought about the weakening of the ties that once bound people together and from which arose vital sources of identity. In consequence, many people now suffer a profound sense of isolation, alienation and meaninglessness. These feelings are expressive of the modern sense of dis-ease. It is the downside of recent change.

More positively, change is helping to bring about significant extensions of personal choice and social diversity. In this sense those who have some economic power have never been so free to differentiate from each other and live in accord with their individually determined values and orientations. Many, especially women, now enjoy previously denied civil rights, public voice and independent wealth, forcing the slow decline of patriarchal structures and attitudes.

Taken together, these trends have had a dual effect, raising both people's sense of insecurity *and* their expectations of personal fulfilment.

Arguably, psychotherapy has been a beneficiary of this contradiction. The very decline of old networks of identity and support through which people could once take collective action or be supported in their life struggles is demanding of people ever more self-reflection and adaptability. We are, in short, seeing the *privatising of distress* and a consequent need for people to seek individualised solutions to today's increasingly complex conditions.

While this is enabling new freedoms there are dangers too. In America, especially, psychotherapy has become identified with personal empowerment. But the concept of 'personal empowerment' can and has on occasion been appropriated to underwrite the ideology of consumerist reward and personal advantage that bedevils advanced capitalism.

There is truth, therefore, in the traditional left-wing objection that psychotherapy displaces the origins of human distress on to the individual, disguising capitalism's structural problems and legitimising its worst social consequences.

However, the traditional left is also wrong. Psychotherapy is an engagement in the field of meaning with the world the person (and the therapist) embodies. Inevitably, it involves a critique of culture. By raising to consciousness personal conditions of oppression and enabling leverage over them it is potentially both subversive of any existing order

and transformative of it in the healthy direction of the satisfaction of human desires.

Importantly, this is what people want. Their desires, expressed with increasing frequency in the practice room, are profoundly corrective of the faults of current society. They are, quite simply, for more intimate relationships and more meaningful lives.

This is a direct and necessary challenge to the growing narcissism of our culture and the profound alienation it engenders: from oneself, from others, from a proper connection between work and value. It requires reconnection of the person in sustaining relationships and a recognition of the influence of societal factors on their well-being as well as those of their personal history and capacities.

Such recognition is radical. It is not 'insight' but 'outsight'. Together, the two raise to consciousness that which requires transformation, and differentiate practically between what is of the individual and of society, enabling a creative interplay between them.

Moreover, the ultimate purpose of this interplay, and so of psychotherapy, is not personal but social and moral. In the final analysis, well-being is not achieved through the unending development of personal capacities but, paradoxically, and through an act of relinquishment; the investment of the self in values that transcend individual advantage, and in consequent actions that have a transforming effect in the world. This confirms what the sages knew. People's maturity and happiness ultimately depends on their concern for others and a living sense of connection to their environment.

Yet the demands of advanced capitalism – which constitute the conditions we live under – are inimical to proper fulfilment and maturity. The pressure, rather, is towards neoteny – the prolonged retention of juvenile characteristics into adulthood – which manifests through and is maintained by the rhetoric of material acquisition and personal advancement on which consumer culture depends. Consider this: the marketing and career possibilities of 'middle youth' as opposed to 'middle age'.

Consciously or not many who seek therapy reject this. They want, quite simply, to grow up; that is, to achieve intimate, interdependent human relationships and to care for others. But they find this difficult in a society that actively does not enable people to do so.

For this reason psychotherapy, if it is to further human well-being, must begin to think politically, and speak beyond the practice room. It must find ways to offer a critique not only of the person, which can isolate the meaning of distress, but of the effects of contemporary culture, especially its will towards juvenility. After all, there is something wrong with a profession so publicly inarticulate about what people are struggling with in their daily lives and the myriad solutions they are creatively attempting for the satisfaction of their human needs.

Unless it does speak out psychotherapy, as a new and developing profession, risks merely reinforcing the ranks of society's 'experts', preoccupied with defining and regulating what is normal and prescribing treatments to reinforce rather than transform it. Then it will become not an act of challenge to existing orders, but one of complicity.

It is this fear, in part, that underlies the rejection of psychotherapy by many educated, creative and politically progressive people today and substantiates charges of a creeping culture of 'therapism' which is sensed, intuitively, to be anti-life, running counter to true human dignity and possibility.

Psychotherapy must therefore begin a constructive discourse with other disciplines and with politicians and policy makers about the direction of contemporary society based on its developing insights into the necessary conditions for well-being. Yet it must also remember its true purpose is not the smooth management of society but, where necessary, its disturbance and subversion.

To forget this would be to deny the broken narratives, dislocated dreams and everyday human distress that emerge in the practice room, and which demand not only personal but profound social change ⊙

Francis Hope is an individual and group psychotherapist who undertakes analyses of cultural trends for businesses.

Do the right thing

The pleasurable life is not the good life: **Roger Scruton** calls for the rediscovery of the link between virtue and happiness.

'The good life' may mean the life that is good for me, or the life that is good *simpliciter*. It is an ancient task of philosophy to show that these things coincide: that happiness and virtue are one. Living in a sceptical age, accepting death as final, and surrounded by available pleasures, modern people have little time for that ancient idea. The good life, they think, is the life of pleasure, in which you get what you want and want what you get. Morality enters the picture; but only because our desires conflict. Morality is the means for avoiding collisions. Obey the moral rules, and you secure the acquiescence of others in the good that you seek for yourself. Disobey the rules, and you give people a motive to obstruct you. Morality limits pleasure, therefore, only in order to promote it.

I do not share that vision of the good life, nor the utilitarian morality that goes with it. Of course, other things being equal, pleasure is always better than the lack of it; but other things are seldom equal. It is not just that pleasures may have harmful consequences – this is familiar enough. It is that they may focus our attention on the wrong things – on the things which undermine our happiness, by diverting our emotions from the course which fulfils us. This, in my view, is what is really wrong with pornography: not that it turns people into sex-criminals, but that it undermines erotic love, and the fulfilment that comes from love. For pornography represents the object of desire as substitutable. Desire becomes a commodity that can be satisfied by anyone with the right equipment, since it is the equipment, not the person, that counts. To view desire in this way, and to practice what pornography preaches, whether alone or in company, is to ruin the erotic life. So, at least, it seems to me.

I take the example because it touches on a vital distinction: that between pleasure and happiness. In his utilitarian frenzy Bentham worried (though not for very long) over the question of whether the pleasures of poetry were superior to the pleasures of pushpin. What concerns me, however, is not the distinction between kinds of pleasure, but the distinction between pleasure and happiness. Pleasure comes with the fulfilment of desire – getting what you want and wanting what you get. Happiness comes with the fulfilment of the person. And much of the moral confusion of our world – a confusion which increases by the day – comes from the fact that we no longer know what happiness is, nor how we might obtain it.

Aristotle made the sensible observation that what is good for a thing depends on what kind of thing it is. What is good for a cat is not necessarily good for an earthworm. To know the good life, we must know what kind of thing we are. And that is where the problems begin. For we seem to belong to two different kinds, each of which defines our essence. We are human beings, with needs, desires and appetites. And we are persons, with goals, ambitions, and ideals. The human being is part of nature, driven by organic processes that resemble those which drive the animals. The person, however, seems to stand above nature, making free and conscious choices which may set him on a collision course with his bodily instincts. Aristotle described human fulfilment (*eudaimonia*, or happiness) in terms which favoured the rational being above the animal. And almost everybody agrees with him. What matters is fulfilment of the person, rather than satisfaction of the body. But what is the relation between people and their bodies? If it is one of identity, how and why do we distinguish personal from animal fulfilment? We know what satisfies the animal: but what fulfils the person? Pornography shows us that such questions are real. So how do we answer them?

Unlike the animals, we are self-conscious. We don't merely do things. We have a conception of what we do and why, and of ourselves as doing it. We cannot avoid judging others, since their actions impinge on our projects, and their characters attract or repel us. Judging others, we judge ourselves. From the habit of judgement comes guilt, and from guilt remorse. We are tangled in the web of moral emotion by our very nature as self-conscious beings. You cannot escape from this web; but you can learn to lie easily in it. And that is the first requirement of the good life: to be what you approve of, and to find in yourself the qualities that you admire in others. Easier said than done, of course; but you can derive from this principle another, of great relevance to life in the modern world: it is not enough to be nice; you have to be good. We are attracted by nice people; but only on the assumption that their niceness is a sign of goodness. When niceness turns out to be a mask, it rather repels than attracts us.

What, you ask, is goodness? The answer is implied in what I have just written. The good qualities are those that we naturally admire – qualities that draw us to others, and which we therefore wish to be credited with ourselves. (We may not wish to possess these qualities, for they involve hard work and sacrifice; but we wish others to believe that we possess them. And of course, if we are rational, we will know that the only reliable way to persuade someone to believe that you are good, is to be good.)

According to Aristotle the naturally admirable qualities are the classical virtues: courage, justice, temperance, wisdom and prudence. Much has changed since classical times, and the qualities we admire depend, at least in part, on the social context. Nevertheless, it was Aristotle's view that rational beings will always admire the cardinal virtues, since people who lack them are unreliable. Even if we accept that, as societies evolve, so too do the qualities that elicit admiration and contempt, there is a core of human virtue that remains unchanged, since it is the core that makes society possible in the first place. Whatever our social circumstances, the cardinal virtues cause us to put our trust in one another, and their absence is disquieting – especially in an emergency.

Emergencies put people to the test. We have lived for a long time without any real emergency – and as a result we have become complacent. From our complacency other and greater emergencies will come, as the environmentalists constantly warn us. But by then it will be too late to rediscover the virtues: they are acquired, as Aristotle pointed out, not by reason but by habit, and the habit must start young. A virtue is a disposition, which leads us to do what is right not by filling our mind with maxims, but by educating our emotions. The virtuous person is not the one who feels no anger, but the one who, as Aristotle puts it, feels the right kind of anger, towards the right object, on the right occasion and in the right degree. (He was thinking, in this connection, of the virtue of justice.)

Why be virtuous? For Aristotle the reason was simple: happiness, he thought, is 'an activity of the soul in accordance with virtue'; hence only the virtuous are happy. And as for the question 'why be happy?', it answers itself, since happiness is the final end, the goal towards which all else is a means. Those somewhat scholastic ideas make little contact with modern culture. If happiness is the goal, why can't you get there by cheating?

Here is one reason why. While you can aim at pleasure, you cannot aim at happiness. You must have other aims – ambitions, goals, values and ideals – with which your personal life is entwined, if you are to be happy. This point, so abundantly illustrated in our literature, is confirmed by philosophy. Happiness comes when you are content with what you have done and with what you are. Happy people look on their goals, their motives, their feelings, and their situation, and see them as intrinsically good. It is impossible therefore that a person should be just happy, and for no reason. Happiness *consists in* something: the achievement of a life's ambition, the repose of requited love, the sense of each day as filled by worthwhile deeds and feelings. So understood, happiness, like love and friendship, comes only when you do not aim at it. There is no shortcut to happiness, since there is no cut to it at all. The one who thinks he can get there by cheating has no real conception of where he is going. You can become wealthy, powerful or successful by cheating; but you cannot become happy. Cheating destroys the perspective on the world which happiness requires – the perspective of the person who lives in self-approval.

There is another consideration that should be borne in mind. Virtuous people have qualities which make them eminently useful to society. They sacrifice themselves for others; they stand up and are counted in the hour of need; they fight off enemies and succour friends; they administer impartial justice; and they are temperate in all their ways, so that long-term commitments come naturally to them. In short, they further the reproduction of society. The converse is true of those whose sole concern is pleasure. They are the natural 'free riders' in any emergency, the people who demand support and protection while being unable and unwilling to give it. They are the people who walk out of their commitments, and who leave children to fend for themselves.

If you enquire into the good life for a dog, then you will quickly conclude that it involves food, exercise, copulation, and all those things which a dog is fitted by nature to do. You will also quickly conclude that these are the very things that enable the dog to reproduce. The good life is the life that reproduces itself.

The same is true of human beings; the difference is that we reproduce not only human life, but also human personality. Now, it is easy to produce new humans; not easy to produce new persons. To reproduce the human person you need parents who take charge of their children, who defend them and nurture them and instil in them the habits which will lead them, in turn, to do the same. You need, in short the life of self-sacrifice which is part of virtue and dependent on virtue for its long-term success. With us too, the good life is the life that reproduces itself. But the reproduction of human life requires not merely that human beings do what is instinctive to them, but that they strive also to be good.

Here we confront an ancient paradox, as real for us as it was for the Greeks who first debated it. It seems that virtuous people are exposed to troubles that the weak-willed, the calculating and the vicious avoid. In battle it is the courageous person who takes the risks, and the coward who comes home to tell the tale. It is the steadfast person who earns the abuse of the mob, and the weak-willed conformist who escapes their censure. It is the honest person who suffers when the villains call in the chips.

But the paradox disappears as soon as we understand the nature of happiness, and its distinction from luck. (How odd, that Latin has the same word – *felicitas* – for both.) You cannot guarantee good luck. But you can ensure that you have the qualities that enable you to survive and prosper without it. These qualities expose us to evils; but the evils are contingent and circumstantial. The courageous person is likely to surmount the dangers which might also destroy him; whatever his luck, he is better placed to emerge from trials in a happy frame of mind than the coward who avoids them. For one thing is certain: the coward will never be proud, as the courageous person is proud, of having survived the danger.

This, it seems to me, is the clue to moral education, as much for us as it was for Aristotle. We cannot guarantee good luck for our children; but we can do our best to ensure that bad luck will not destroy them. And this means inculcating the dispositions which lead of their own accord to fulfilment, and which expose us to troubles only by giving us the means to overcome them. These dispositions are the virtues.

The great question that lies before all of us, is whether the cultivation of virtue will continue, in an age of dwindling religious faith. Even if Aristotle is right in thinking that we all have reason to cultivate virtue, his argument is beyond the reach of most people. What therefore will inspire them to do what they should?

You can see religion in much the way that Plato saw the 'Noble Lie' – the myth told to the people, that would motivate them to do what they would otherwise not do, even though it is in their interests to do it. But that is not the only way to see it. We are entangled by nature in a web of moral feeling; we do not escape from it by selfishness, and the pursuit of purchasable pleasures only makes it worse. We must learn, therefore, to focus our thoughts and our emotions on those things which earn the good opinion of the people who know us: helping and giving to others, protecting and educating the young, confronting and admonishing evil, and, above all these and radiating through them, living in 'natural piety'. And we must recognise that, in doing this, our self-opinion may also mislead us, and that we must atone for

Things ill done, and done to others' harm,
Which once we took for exercise of virtue.

We admire those who live penitentially, and spontaneously forgive them their faults. And what we admire in others, we need in ourselves.

By striving to deserve the good opinion of those who know us, we may also earn the hatred and contempt of those who do not. This is perhaps the most important of life's lessons, and the hardest to bear. That is why steadfastness is a virtue, and why we should teach it to our children. For no one can be assured of happiness, until learning to distance themselves from anger that is undeserved, and to continue nevertheless in the course of action that provoked it ⊙

Roger Scruton is a philosopher, critic, journalist and novelist. His latest book is An Intelligent Person's Guide to Popular Culture (1998).

Part 2

Questioning the good life

Do we mind the gap?

Inequality in Britain is greater than in any other major European country. **Will Hutton** argues that this has dangerous consequences for the good life of all citizens and challenges government to act now.

There are now London sandwich shops that compete to sell extravagant £7 school lunch boxes; at lunch the kids compare whether they have ciabatta bread or the humbler rations provided by income support. In the premier league TV largesse is enabling the rich football clubs to open up an unbridgeable gap in talent with the smaller clubs as they buy up the best players. The life expectancy of the top ten per cent of income earners is rising; the life expectancy of the bottom 10 per cent is stagnating.

We think of inequality almost wholly in terms of differences in income and to a lesser extent of opportunity, but in truth the impact of the unequal society is pervasive. It is manifest in children's envy and sense of injustice in the classroom as classmates get out their lunch boxes. It is present in the careless selling of football clubs to television companies and the transmutation of fans into commodities. It is reflected in the prospect of a happy and healthy retirement for some and not for others. Inequality and its effects are all around us, and they undermine the ideal of the good life.

But against this background the Labour party no longer chooses to argue for lower inequality and more redistribution of income and wealth; the prime minister is openly dismissive of such an approach. All that is permitted is the softer language of promoting fairness and individual opportunity. Many Blairites regard this as another long overdue ditching of ridiculous baggage from old Labour's past; they are wrong. It is the surrender of a core value that not only defines the left of centre and its politics, but is one of the building blocks of any good society. After all, it was not Marx but Plato who said that equality leads to friendship. There is a trinity of values that underpin western democratic civilisation: liberty, equality and fraternity. To accept the Conservative hierarchy of values in which equality has little or no place, as New Labour is in danger of doing, is to turn its back on its tradition and its responsibility to the democratic process. Who is to argue for more equality in our democracy if not the left?

The facts about the deep inequalities in access to the resources needed for a decent life are briefly summarised. Average incomes between 1979 and 1997 have grown by 44 per cent in real terms after allowing for housing costs, but the highest tenth of earners enjoyed an increase of 70 per cent. By contrast the poorest tenth of the population have suffered a cut in real income of 9 per cent. The proportion of people living on an income of less than half the average – the nearest thing to an official poverty line – has risen to 24 per cent. Side by side with this development is the emergence of a new overclass whose incomes are staggering: for example, half the directors of Britain's top 100 companies earn more than £600,000 and that is before the impact of bonus schemes and share options. Similar earnings are available throughout the City. The growth in income inequality in Britain has been so rapid that we now have the highest level of inequality of any major European country and are near the top of the indsutrialised world's ranking.

This widening gap between rich and poor is reflected in a myriad of ways. There is access to education, with expensive private schools producing disproportionately good examination results and access to university. There is the experience of good health, not merely because of diet and housing but, as Richard Wilkinson of the University of Sussex has explained, because of the way in which high and low self-worth is so closely associated with earning power. The lower our earnings in relation to the average, the lower our self-esteem and the poorer our health.

Inequality, in short, penetrates to the very heart of our society and undermines the prospects of a satisfying and decent life for the many. It breaks down trust relationships and undermines our capacity to empathise with others. This is because the human experience is essentially social. We do not live as islands; we seek and offer each other's good opinion as the basic fuel of human intercourse. The expectation and need for reciprocity is a more generalised human need; it underpins friendship and trust. It is at the core of our conceptions of social capital without which our societies begin to become unhinged.

Yet the wholly unequal society undermines such capacity for affinity. It so shrinks the common public and social spaces in which human beings interact that it impoverishes the common language and moral codes we use to understand and deal with each other. Building friendships becomes harder between people whose status and income varies hugely; and friendship is a basic emotional need. The poorer are even constrained in their capacity to socialise because they do not have the wherewithal.

And because we can comprehend each other increasingly poorly, we risk losing the capacity to empathise and to trust. The circle shrinks among whom we seek a good reputation; we are less and less endangered by anger and fearful of jealousy. We become less capable of being shamed. The ties and expectations of reciprocity diminish. It is not surprising that Richard Wilkinson demonstrates that more unequal societies are those with higher suicide rates, less trust and more violence than those with more even distributions of income and wealth. He quotes James Gillian, a prison psychiatrist, writing of violence: 'I have yet to see a serious act of violence that was not provoked by the experience of being shamed and humiliated, disrespected and ridiculed, and did not represent the attempt to prevent or undo this loss of face – no matter how severe the punishment'.[1]

As well as exacerbating these psychological and emotional ills, inequality is also economically and socially *inefficient*. The unequal society is an unhealthy society with poor housing, high levels of unemployment and social exclusion; it requires high public expenditure to redress these imbalances and disfigurements. The unequal company is one where teams are hard to build and motivation difficult to sustain; Japanese companies' anxiety to place a limit on the difference between the pay of senior executives and shopfloor workers is not idiosyncratic, but has been essential to establishing the common ethic which is the foundation of their corporate success.

The unequal country with rich cities and poor regions finds it hard to grow and develop itself; the structures, institutions and policies appropriate for the rich areas are wholly inappropriate for the poor parts. The unequal economy is hard to manage economically; its economic cycles are more violent as the poor and insecure move from being workers and consumers, swelling the boom, to social security

1 Williamson R, 1998, 'Why inequality is bad for you', *Marxism Today*, special issue, October 1998; Williamson R, 1996, *Unhealthy Societies: The affliction of inequality*, Routledge, London.

dependants intensifying the downturn. The spending and taxation policies appropriate for the rich regions are inappropriate for the poor regions.

Inequality, in short, is pernicious. To argue that is not to argue for absolute equality any more than one argues for absolute liberty. There are plainly delicate trade-offs and compromises. But unless politicians develop a story about why inequality matters to us all, there is little chance of building the coalition needed to redress it – whether raising marginal tax rates, reducing the privileges of private schools or sustaining the health service. And as the value attached to equality diminishes, we are all diminished. The premier league becomes more unfair and our capacity to make friends alike are reduced. New Labour's refusal so far openly to face this issue could prove to be its Achilles heel; both in achieving what it wants to accomplish in power, and in sustaining its support in the country. The people want a more equal society. The Labour party will be scorned if it does not respond ⊙

Will Hutton is Editor-in-Chief of the Observer, *and the author of several books including* The State We Are In *(Jonathan Cape, 1995) and* The State to Come *(Vintage, 1997).*

A modest proposal against inequality

Bob Holman

Since the reign of Margaret Thatcher, the institution of the so-called free market and the motivation of personal greed have dominated Britain. Undoubtedly, one outcome has been huge material gains for many, which are seen as providing 'the good life'.

But there is a flip side. An inevitable by-product of almost unfettered capitalism has been a dramatic rise in poverty and inequality. Between 1979 and 1990, the number of people with incomes below half the national average income increased from 5 million to 13 million. Most poor parents struggle hard to make satisfying lives for their families. Nonetheless, poverty is associated with hardship, distress and family insecurity. I have recently edited the writings of seven residents of the Easterhouse estate in Glasgow. One named Anita wrote: 'I don't think I can cope much longer. Yesterday I had nothing at all for my kids to eat and I called the social worker but it was just a blunt "no".'[1] Some good life!

Lives are spoilt not just by the hardships of poverty but also by the impact of inequality.

Professor Richard Wilkinson concludes, from a great number of studies, that in countries where sections of the population enjoy great material success, those at the bottom deem themselves as rejects and failures.[2] There feelings are then internalised to stimulate apathy, illness and even suicide. Erica, another of the Easterhouse women, had gone to bed cold because she could not afford heating. The next day she wrote in her diary, 'I didn't even want to get up today because I felt so fed up with my life. It's the same thing, day in, day out.' Some good life!

The risk of riches

Will Hutton identifies the winners in wealthy Britain as the top 40 per cent with high incomes, spacious homes and private pensions.[3] They appear to have everything. Yet their concentration on material gain can have its drawbacks. Elsewhere, I refer to examples like the financier who earns £625,000 a year and whose greatest joy is making deals about which he said, 'I feel so good; there's nothing like it.' Meanwhile, he rarely saw his chil-

1 Holman B et al, 1998, *Faith in the poor*, Lion Publishing, Oxford.
2 Wilkinson R, 1994, *Unfair shares*, Barnardos, London.
3 Hutton W, 1995, *The state we're in*, Jonathan Cape, London.

dren in the evenings and was too busy even to spend the summer and Christmas holidays with them.[4] Money becomes an end in itself to be displayed by spending lavishly on homes, clothes, music, sport and so on. Of course, used in moderation, the latter are all activities which can facilitate human relationships. Unfortunately, money has become a god and consumer items its idols. Their devotees then have less space for families, little regard for those in social need and not time for a spiritual dimension to their lives. I don't accept this as the good life.

The good life and equality

I write as a Christian and I take seriously Christ's injunction that we should love God and love our neighbour as ourselves. I acknowledge that many readers will not accept my beliefs but I hope that their religion or humanity will lead them in a similar direction. My understanding of the good life is one in which individuals enjoy sufficient but not excessive material and social goods, in which they love those nearest to them and in which they act unselfishly towards other citizens. This kind of life cannot be fully attained while the spirit of personal greed holds sway. It requires a more equal society. By

equality I am not advocating a nation of look-alike robots who receive exactly the same income. Rather, I see it as a society in which members are driven by a sense of mutuality, that is, an acceptance of obligations towards others, so that resources are distributed so as not to place any citizen at severe social and material disadvantage.

I advocate equality for these reasons:

● I believe that God created all individuals as of unique and equal value. It follows that all have equal claim to the resources and opportunities that contribute to the good life.
● I find it unfair that, for instance, Ann Gloag of Stagecoach can spend £1.5 million on furnishing her castle while an Easterhouse woman cannot afford a washing machine for her family. I find it obscene that Gordon Brown can spend more on a haircut than some families receive or earn in a week.
● I reckon that greater equality will enhance, not restrict, individual freedom. Youngsters whose potential is hindered by social depriva-

4 Holman B, 1997, *Towards equality*, SPCK, London.

tions would have a greater chance of developing their abilities. Simultaneously, those whose lives are currently taken over by possession may find richer satisfactions in interacting with people rather than things – or even by relating to the Creator.

● I anticipate that great equality will break down barriers of class, race, gender, age and location and so lead to a greater experience of fellowship.

Towards equality

Egalitarians often meet with the response, 'Such change is impossible. Human beings are just concerned with themselves.' Certainly, New Labour has been unwilling to challenge the rule of capitalism and the values that bolster it. Yet social values and individual practice can change. In 1939, Britain was governed by a government devoted to the free market and to cuts in public expenditure. In the same year, when I was one of millions evacuated because of the war, it was within a nation where the Poor Law still held sway. Yet that war stimulated changes in public attitudes so that many people wanted to accept sacrifices for the sake of others. The outcome was a post-war Labour government that, despite overwhelming economic difficulties, established the welfare state, promoted full employment and reduced inequality.

So change is possible. It is in order to talk of a government that could legislate both for a maximum income as well as a minimum one. It is practical to plan for a society in which public values are so different that poverty is abolished, class barriers removed and resources distributed to facilitate a good life for all. The question then is how can greater equality be pursued? I don't pretend to have the answers but I can suggest two paths we can tread.

Too often, those who mouth the case for equality do not practice it. Roy Hattersley, when an MP, managed to fervently attack inequality while himself enjoying outside earning of £100,000. He now expresses his egalitarian sentiments as a member of the House of Lords. Such hypocrisy does harm. By contrast, those who live out their beliefs become models that others will follow. Those in the present top 40 per cent, including Labour MPs, could set the pace by:

● refusing incomes above the national average, and

- living alongside those in greatest need, sending their children to local schools and acting in ways that reduce social divisions and promote social unity.

Alfred Salter was a brilliant doctor and later an MP who chose to work and live in Bermondsey. His biographer, Fenner Brockway, concluded: 'Thousands of men and women learned to have a new faith in humanity because they saw in him the promise of what the good life might be.'[5] Values are best spread by those who put them into action.

Whether in the top 40 per cent, the middle 30 per cent or the bottom 30 per cent, all citizens can identify with organisations that convey the values of equality. Neighbourhood groups are locally controlled projects that, particularly in deprived areas, run food co-ops, credit unions, youth activities, holiday schemes and so on. They have over 2,500,000 participants and are relevant to low-income residents for three reasons. First, they are practical, offering low credit, cheap food, holidays and the like. They do not remove poverty but they do alleviate it. Second, they involve low-income people in positions of responsibility and so help to counter the feelings of powerlessness and failure associated with inequality. Third, they convey the principles and practices of sharing, self-sacrifice and collective action that must be the foundations of the good life.

Neighbourhood groups are usually short of funds. The Labour government should establish a National Neighbourhood Fund to ensure their continuance and expansion. This would then spread services that are directly helpful to the bottom 30 per cent in the present and bolster values that can stimulate an equality for the future. But it is not enough to wait for the future. The best way towards the good life for all is by more people attempting to live the good life now ⊙

Bob Holman is a neighbourhood worker in Easterhouse, Glasgow.

5 Brockway F, 1995, *Bermondsey story: the life of Alfred Salter*, Stephen Humphrey, London.

A Grossly Distorted Picture

Gross Domestic Product is the key indicator of economic progress. But **Alex MacGillivray** says it tells us all too little about real progress and well-being.

Growth for growth's sake, not for the good life

Gordon Brown has finally set the date for getting married. His best man might be tempted to tell the rather old economists' joke about the man who marries his housekeeper, and causes a fall in GDP. He shouldn't tell it, though. Not many people will get it. 'GDP? What does *that* stand for?'

Gross Domestic Product is a puzzling phenomenon. What other secret weapon invented by the Allies to help win the Second World War has proved so obscure and yet so enduring? The atomic bomb, Colonel Bogey, radar, Spam – all have had their heyday and are now being put out to grass. So what can explain the longevity of GDP?

GDP is undoubtedly the most influential decision-making tool in the world. It has dictated the economic, social and environmental policies of most countries for most of the time since the 1950s. Yet it is hardly a 'headline' indicator in the conventional sense.

When most people argue about the good life, they fall back on indicators like the length of hospital waiting lists, unemployment rates, pupil-teacher ratios or the alarming rise in childhood asthma. These are the sorts of headline indicators that the Government is currently developing. But you are not likely to overhear your neighbours disputing whether the GDP growth rate should be 2.5 or 3 per cent.

It is not that people have no interest in economics. Many people assiduously track exchange rate fluctuations and even the FTSE index, yet hardly anyone even knows what GDP stands for, let alone what its value was last year, or by how much it is predicted to grow this year. How is it that what is held to be the most important indicator in the world remains a mystery to most people?

It is not as though GDP is very complicated to understand. We simply add up every single financial transaction that take place in the country over the year. Subtract the intermediary deals to avoid double-counting along the production chain. Thus we count the sale of the loaf to the customer by the baker but ignore the sale of the flour by the miller to the baker. That is GDP. It is far from being rocket science.

No, the problem is not that GDP is inherently boring or beyond human understanding. It is a headline indicator of severely restricted interest because most people don't need to know much about economic growth and how it is measured. Conviction about its importance is so deeply engrained that support for increasing levels of GDP is taken as axiomatic. Politicians, civil servants and business people, we assume, will do everything in their power to promote economic growth – *because they believe it is the motor propelling us towards the good life.*

The trouble is, this motor has broken down.

GDP and quality of life indicators

Those in the know realise just how indiscriminate GDP really is as an indicator. The supposed engine of quality of life, it does little to guide our understanding of how much our well-being is improved by economic growth. Money transactions include a whole host of things that add little or nothing to well-being, like repairing the damage incurred by a car crash. Conversely, some things do add to quality of life but have no value in the conventional market – like household work and child-care by parents. That explains the old joke about the man and his house-keeper – once they got married, he didn't have to pay her, so GDP fell. Get it?

To make matters worse, some of our activities add to *current* growth (such as oil consumption) but will incur *future* costs (for example, coping with storms and flooding as a result of global warming fuelled by oil consumption).

For all these reasons, *The Economist* has called GDP a 'Grossly Distorted Picture'. The hidden costs of environmental degradation and social exclusion, as well as the invisible benefits of unpaid work, make it an incredibly misleading indicator. In fact, it was never intended to measure the good life in the first place. 'The welfare of a nation can scarcely be inferred from a measurement of national income', warned Nobel Laureate Simon Kuznets, the architect of GDP. 'Goals for growth should specify more growth *of* what and *for* what.'

Ten years ago, a theologian, his son and a World Bank economist (John and Clifford Cobb, and Herman Daly) finally listened and decided to overhaul GDP. They devised the Index of Sustainable Economic Welfare (ISEW, pronounced 'I sue'). The ISEW is calculated for the USA by adding and subtracting a range of costed social and environmental factors to personal consumption. The result showed a dramatic story – while the size of the US economy has grown steadily since the 1950s, levels of overall economic, social and environmental welfare faltered in the 1970s and haven't climbed significantly since then.

Earlier this year, a full technical report on a British ISEW was launched by the New Economics Foundation.[1] This builds on developmental work undertaken at the University of Surrey and elsewhere since 1994. It graphically demonstrates how economic policy since the 1950s has ridden roughshod over the environment, and has ignored deteriorating social conditions. In fact, the index shows that there has hardly been any *overall* improvement in welfare since the 1950s: rising material standards of living for many individuals have to be balanced against a decline in common goods – lower environmental quality, rising crime levels and higher rates of unemployment and insecurity.

We have argued that the ISEW is a far better indicator of the overall state of our quality of life than Gross Domestic Product. It would make a good candidate for the new headline measure of national progress that Labour promised before they came to power. But civil servants have argued that the ISEW is based on too many arbitrary assumptions and, perish the thought, 'value judgements'. The result? We remain stuck with GDP, even though everyone concedes it is a hopeless gauge of progress towards the good life.

But an alternative economic indicator doesn't have to be the arbitrary plaything of policy wonks. The New Economics Foundation, Friends of the Earth and the Centre for Environmental Strategy at Surrey University have launched on the world wide web an interactive version of the famous ISEW index, which encourages ordinary people to make the value judgements that do – and should – govern policy.

Visitors to this innovative web site do not even need to know what GDP stands for to have their say. Now *you* have the opportunity to tell policy-makers what you will stand for. How much air pollution can your family put up with? Do you tolerate extremes of wealth and poverty, or would you prefer more equality? How valuable do you think the work

1 Jackson T, Marks N, Ralls J, Stymne S, 1998, *Sustainable Economic Welfare in the UK 1950-1996*, New Economics Foundation/Centre for Environmental Strategy, London.

done by women in the home is? At last, here is the chance to let civil servants and economists addicted to a business-as-usual vision of economic development know what you want.[2]

The web site gives users the chance to make ten important adjustments to GDP, based on their own best judgements. The result will be an Index of Sustainable Economic Welfare that reflects popular views – and is therefore as robust as any indicator can be. It will be used to persuade the Government that there is no excuse to stick with the misleading GDP indicator as a yardstick of progress.

It could be that the message is getting through already at the highest levels. As Gordon Brown shrewdly said in his pre-budget statement on environmental taxation, *'Quality of growth matters; not just quantity'*. In the quest for the true good life, size isn't everything ☉

Alex MacGillivray is Research Manager at the New Economics Foundation.

2 Readers are urged to visit the ISEW web site at *http://www.foe.co. uk/progress.*

Runaway world

The West has entered an age of unparalleled material abundance. **David Goldblatt** argues that our version of the good life is unsustainable in an era of globalisation and ecological threats.

'We do not want to enter the age of abundance only to find that we have lost the values that might teach us how to enjoy it.'
Richard Crossland, *The Future of Socialism*[1]

At the end of the twentieth century it is surely clear that in the West, despite enduring social exclusion and relative poverty, we have entered 'the age of abundance'. If we ever possessed the values and practices that would teach us to enjoy it, they are currently in desperately short supply. In the four decades since Crossland wrote the above words, global economic output has roughly quadrupled and a hugely disproportionate volume of that output has been, and still is, consumed by the populations of the West: the richest 20 per cent of the world account for 86 per cent of expenditure on personal consumption.[2] We live by any contemporary or historical standards in extraordinarily wealthy societies.

It is equally clear that the acquisition of material abundance has yet to yield an equal advance in the sum of human *happiness*; unless of course your idea of human happiness includes unfulfillable aspirations, uncontrollably exaggerated insecurities, eating disorders, stress-related disease, addictions and substance abuse of various kinds, working longer hours, seeing less of your friends and family, sitting in traffic jams – and so on. In the midst of a global financial implosion, these dilemmas may seem to be luxurious pathologies to many Russians or Indonesians, but they remain central to the experience of many people in the West. Moreover, the affluence and abun-

1 C.A.R. Crossland, 1956, *The Future of Socialism*, Jonathan Cape, London, 529.
2 UNDP, 1998, *Human Development Report*, OUP, Oxford.

dance that spawns them are the aspiration of almost all of the developing world.

The dominant political projects of the twentieth century – left and right, democratic and authoritarian – have no convincing answers to these dilemmas. In part, this is because they have all shared the assumption that, if we could sufficiently raise our levels of output, production and consumption – by whatever means – then a multiplicity of good things would follow: faster growth, higher wages, bigger profits, more goods, newer services, happy people. As a consequence these projects have had a great deal to say about the *efficient economy*, but precious little to say about the *good life*. It has been assumed that the latter would, under certain important conditions, follow from the former. So, for example, one of the central tasks of liberal political theory, in its most libertarian guise, has been to specify how to create a society in which individual aspirations, projects and desires can be freely chosen and pursued, checked only by the rights of others do to the same. In its Rawlsian form liberalism has sought to balance these liberties with a measure of justice sufficient to ensure that no one is excluded from making these choices by lack of access to a minimal set of resources. What people then choose to do with those resources and how they live their lives is not a matter for politicians or theorists.

Socialists and social democrats may have disagreed with liberals over where the balance lay between liberty and equality, and argued for a more fulsome conception of the minimal conditions of effective autonomy, but they have been equally chary of enquiring into how abundance and autonomy can be converted into a rewarding life. Crossland's note of uncertainty comes at the end of over five hundred pages on the economics and politics of growth, modernisation and redistribution. Conservatives and communists have been less reticent in pronouncing on the content of the good life, but given the narrowness and paucity of their respective visions and their authoritarian overtones, one wishes that they had been more so. In that respect, at any rate, liberalism's separation of the public and the private, the creation of the good society and the pursuit of the good life, remains a considerable achievement.

The environmental movement has mounted a sharp and increasingly potent challenge to these ideas. It has broken with the dominant projects of the past century and their treatment of the good life in three ways. First, environmentalists have argued that the simple equation

between abundance and the good life is flawed. Abundance and affluence bring their own problems. A good life is something greater than
the sum of what we can manage to consume before we die.

Second, environmentalists have argued that the pursuit of material abundance by some acts as a significant check on the capacity of
many others to pursue a good life. Third, they have dared to suggest
that some of the substantive content of the notion of the good life
is a matter for collective discussion rather than individual choice
alone. The creation of a good society, which at the very least would
be an *ecologically sustainable* society, may only be possible if there is a
wholesale redefinition by individuals of their own conception and
practice of the good life. In these arguments lie both the enormous
potential appeal – and perhaps also the fatal limitations – of modern
environmentalism.

Environmentalists are hardly the first people to argue that more
money doesn't make you happy. *But it is unique for a social movement or
a political project to make this argument so central to its concerns.* The reasons
for this are complex, but it seems clear that a politics so attuned to the
destruction of an uncommodified nature, of priceless ecosystems and
of inestimable wealth, should also be sharply attuned to the parallel
processes of the corrosion and destruction of the self and community.
This capacity to oppose the commodification and fragmentation of
both the natural environment and the social world is a potent political asset. Beneath the swirling froth of advertising industry imagery
and a quotidian culture of consumerism there is, amongst part of the
Western publics, a largely subterranean but deep current of support
for a politics of restraint and repair, of limits, of 'enough is enough'.
This is a rich if under-worked seam for a politics of the good life that
is based on the *qualitative texture of experience* rather than the quantita-
tive accumulation of things.

The second environmentalist argument is well known and can be
simply explained. The quadrupling of global economic output in the
post-war era has been accompanied by an historically unprecedented
rise in the scale, scope and complexity of environmental degradation
and the unsustainable consumption of potentially renewable resources.
This has been driven by a relentless rise in global population, and by
the OECD world's 50-year orgy of consumption, combined with the
relentless global spread of industrialisation under the aegis of both
communism and capitalism. Along with the air-conditioned station-

wagon, incredibly expensive nuclear energy, a rapid expansion in the salty snack industry and the cheapness of disposable razors, this concatenation of events has brought us accelerated global warming, ozone depletion, massive species loss, acid rain, radioactive estuaries, water shortages, widespread land degradation, the collapse of fisheries and so on, *ad infinitum*. While even the most affluent cannot escape every externality and insecurity that these environmental problems bring, there seems little doubt that the costs and threats imposed by global environmental degradation are unequally shared within and between nations. The side effects of one small part of the planet pursuing one interpretation of the good life are making it increasingly difficult for others, those living and those yet to arrive, to pursue a potentially satisfying life at all.

Given the extent to which both the endless pursuit of economic abundance threatens our own and future generations' environmental security, and given the increasingly obvious dissociation between that project and the creation of balanced, fulfilling lives, is it not surprising that Western environmental politics has had so few electoral, if not regulatory, achievements? Most OECD countries can boast a plethora of environmental legislation, ministries, mission statements and plans, but none can point to a sustained and important period of environmentalism in national government, national elections fought decisively on environmental issues or a sustained and integrated attack on the environmental and social pathologies of over-consumption. Of course, the range of vested interests opposed to the environmentalist project is enormous. The immediate beneficiaries of many environmental policies are often political minnows compared to the immediate losers; the transitional costs of environmental improvements outweigh the contemporary benefits; future gains cannot be reaped now and future generations have no vote. In any case, Green parties have been victim to their own inexperience and predilection for internal conflict.

But more fundamental to explaining this political underachievement is the fate of the third argument; that we will only curb our voracious environmental appetites and have the opportunity to cultivate alternative sources of the good life if we are prepared collectively and individually to re-evaluate the meaning of wealth and well-being. The main lines of that revaluation are well known: consume less but consume better; work less and live more; trade increasing income for more free time; value durability over novelty. My question is not what combination of rhetoric and idiom, practice and policy could mobilise mass support behind such a project – though we shall hardly get very far without considering this – but why it is such a necessary task? Not everyone would accept the necessity of such a cultural revolution.

Market optimists believe that with a sufficiently accurate pricing policy, environmentally destructive behaviour can be curbed. Self-interest can be turned to environmental ends. Ecological pessimists might argue that as the consequences of environmental degradation become more obvious and more pressing locally and globally, self-interest will persuade Western publics to vote for much more radical programmes of economic and ecological reform. Both of these strategies are of course important. No successful green politics will be implemented in the absence of significant market reregulation and, unpalatable as it is, few major political victories can be won in the absence of more disasters on the scale of Chernobyl or Bhopal.

However, both strategies are by themselves, or even in combination, inadequate given the scale of environmental reform that is required and the shockingly short timescales in which they need to be implemented. Is it possible, for example, that merely by altering the relative costs and benefits of different modes of transport, we could achieve a massive decline in car use? Can the transformation of the transport infrastructure triumph over a culture in which cars, along with more mundane issues of movement, are used to express identities, boost egos and support a phenomenal industry of publishing and paraphernalia? Is it wise, given what we know about the unpredictability and irreversibility of environmental change, to sit back and wait for the crisis to come? How much more evidence do the unconvinced, the uninterested, the selfish and the lazy require? It seems to me that the prospects for environmentally induced global social dislocation and conflicts are right here, right now. But until our sense of the good, of our own well-being, can be at least partially disengaged from the consumption of objects and re-engaged with at least some of the rest of humanity – like our grandchildren, for example – we are unlikely to move on either of these issues.

Ironically enough, the role of alternative visions of the good life in restraining the environmental appetite may be similar to that suggested by Max Weber for the Protestant Ethic in shaping and promoting capitalism: 'Not ideas, but material and ideal interests directly govern conduct... Yet very frequently the world images created by ideas have, like switchmen, determined the tracks along which action has been pushed by the dynamic of interest'.[3] There is in much of the West and also in the developing world a 'dynamic of material interest' in environmental protection and of 'ideal interest' in coping with the pathologies of affluence. What we do not have yet are the world images of the good life that can switch their direction. If we fail to find them it is more likely than not that we shall collectively fly off the tracks together ⊙

David Goldblatt is a Lecturer at the Faculty of Social Sciences, The Open University. He is hoping to live a good life in the near future rather than write about it.

3 M. Weber, 1970, "The Social Psychology of the World Religions", in H. Gerth and C. Wright Mills (eds), *From Max Weber: Essays in Sociology*, RKP, London, p280.

Think global, buy local

Helena Norberg-Hodge and **Adrian Henriques**
argue that globalising trends must be challenged: more
localised economies are a key to better lives for all.

There is no definitive view of the 'good life', but very often it combines
contact with nature, healthy relations with family and friends,
freedom and perhaps particularly ease. Such a vision of the good life
is one which very many people can understand and share: it peers out
at us from advertisements for holidays, Karl Marx seemed to share such
a view in his vision for the Communist society – even Aristotle wrote
of it in similar terms. Yet just as widely shared is the belief that, today,
all this is simply not possible. Whatever else progress means, it also
seems to mean moving further away from the good life in most practical ways. So we all yearn for it, but how many of us can live it?

Despite this, there are a few societies which retain many of the characteristics of the good life, even today. One such example is Ladakh,
in northern India. Due to its physical isolation, Ladakh has only relatively recently been open to Western and to market influences. It was
a subsistence society, traditionally governed at the family and local community level. It was very sparsely populated and people appeared to
be simply happy. Since Ladakh has been opened to the world economy,
however, there have been profound changes which threaten the heart
of this society. Some of the key changes are increasing conflict, family
disruption, abandonment of the local culture and environmental
decay. This is not an unusual pattern of development in the South, or
in the industrialised North.

So even if the vision of the good life is widely shared, the world as
a whole appears able to provide such a life for fewer and fewer people.
An increasing proportion of the population is living in towns and the

disparities in wealth are growing. People are leaving or being thrown off the land in many countries.

The experience of Ladakh suggests that economic progress is responsible for the degradation of society and people's dissatisfaction with life. This article argues that the movement away from the good life is driven by the kind of economic progress that depends on ever-increasing scale. As a result, there are a wide range of policy measures that could be adopted to mitigate the adverse effects of economic development without sacrificing material gains. The key is to focus resources on local economies and emerging local initiatives, instead of on the global economy and on trade.

International policies

Today governments of every type are embracing policies that promote liberalisation and an opening up to economic globalisation in the belief that they are both inevitable and will cure their ailing economies. Yet globalisation is not inevitable – most governments are actively encouraging it. One of the main international policy thrusts responsible is that of 'free trade', which has given rise to the World Trade Organisation.

In fact, a careful policy of using trade tariffs to regulate the import of goods which could be produced locally would be in the best interests of the majority. Such 'protectionism' is not aimed at fellow citizens in other countries; rather, it is a way of safeguarding jobs and defending local resources against the excessive power of transnational corporations. Countries in the South, and increasingly in the North, are being hit hard by free trade agreements like GATT and NAFTA. Contrary to the aim of such treaties, they would be far better off, if they were allowed to protect and conserve their natural resources, nurture national and local business enterprises, and limit the impact of foreign media and advertising on their culture. Even 'fair trade' may not always be in the long-term interest of the majority in the South since it can pull people away from a relatively secure local economy and put them on the bottom rung of the global economic ladder.

Another international policy thrust responsible for globalisation is the drive for a free flow of capital, which may be embodied in the Multilateral Agreement on Investment. Capital flows have been necessary for the growth of transnational corporations. Their ability to shift profits, operating costs and investment capital to and from all of their national operations enables them to operate anywhere in the world, and even to hold sovereign nations hostage by threatening to leave and take their jobs with them. A company providing several hundred jobs can expect to be offered capital grants for its building and machinery costs, low-interest loans, subsidised training for its new labour force and a host of tax relief measures.

Small local businesses, given no such subsidies, cannot hope to survive such competition. Limiting the free flow of capital would help to reduce the advantage that huge corporations have over smaller, more local enterprises, and help to make corporations more accountable to the places in which they operate.

National policies

At the national level, policies actively discriminate against small-scale enterprise in many ways. This is not usually intentional: it has perhaps seemed more efficient to manage and encourage large-scale enterprise. Yet in almost every country tax regulations discriminate against small businesses. Small-scale production is usually more labour-intensive, and heavy taxes are levied on labour through income taxes, social welfare taxes, value-added taxes, payroll taxes and the like. Meanwhile, tax breaks such as accelerated depreciation, investment allowances and tax credits are afforded the capital- and energy-intensive technologies used by large corporate producers.

Reversing, or even neutralising, this bias in the tax system would not only help local economies but would create more jobs by favouring people instead of machines. Similarly, taxes on the energy used in production would encourage businesses that are less dependent on high levels of technological input – which again means smaller, more labour-intensive enterprises. If petrol and diesel fuel were taxed so that the price reflected their real costs – including some measure of the environmental damage their consumption causes – there would be a reduction in transport, an increase in regional production for local consumption and a healthy diversification of the economy.

Small businesses are discriminated against through the lending policies of banks, which charge them significantly higher interest rates for loans than they charge big firms. They also often require that small business owners personally guarantee their loans – a guarantee not sought from the directors of large businesses.

Perhaps more insidiously, an unfair burden often falls on small-scale enterprises through regulations aimed at problems caused by large-scale production. Battery-style chicken farms, for example, clearly need significant environmental and health regulations. The millions of closely kept animals are highly prone to disease, tons of concentrated effluent need to be safely disposed of, and long-distance transport of chickens entails the risk of spoilage. Yet a small producer – such as a farmer with a dozen free-range chickens – is subject to essentially the same regulations, often raising costs to levels that can make it impossible to remain in business. Such discriminatory regulations are widespread. Again, a local entrepreneur wanting to bake cakes at home to sell at local shops will in most cases need to install an industrial kitchen to meet health regulations – making it economically impossible to succeed.

Local and regional land use regulations could be greatly strengthened to protect wild areas, open space and farmland from development. Political and financial support could be given to the various forms of land trusts that have been designed for this purpose. In the United States, there are now over 900 such trusts protecting more than 2.7 million acres of land. In some cases, local governments have used public money to buy the development rights to farmland, thereby simultaneously protecting the land from suburban sprawl while reducing the financial pressure on farmers. Studies have also shown that developed land can cost local governments significantly more in services than the extra tax revenues generated – meaning that when land is developed, taxpayers not only lose the benefits of open space, they lose money as well.

In urban areas, zoning regulations usually segregate residential, business and manufacturing areas – a restriction necessitated by the needs and hazards of large-scale production. These could be changed to enable an integration of homes, small shops and small-scale production. A rethinking of restrictions on community-based ways of living would also be beneficial: zoning and other regulations aimed at limiting high-density developments often end up prohibiting environmentally sound living arrangements like eco-housing and eco-villages.

Investing in scale

Conventional economic theory suggests that to build an economy in the fastest way, the state should invest in fundamental infrastructure which can support large-scale industrialisation. This is the same as subsidising globalisation. The money currently spent on long-distance road transport, for example, offers an idea of how heavily subsidised the global economy is. In the United States, where there are about 2.5 million miles of paved roads, another $80 billion has been earmarked for highways in the next few years – and plans are even being considered for a road link between Alaska and Siberia. The European Community, meanwhile, is planning to spend $120 billion ecus to add an additional 7,500 miles of superhighways to Western Europe by 2002, and is considering a tunnel to connect Europe with Africa. Throughout the South, scarce resources are similarly being spent. In New Guinea, for example, $48 million was spent on 23 miles of roads to bring logs to the export market.

Shifting such support towards a range of transport options that favour smaller, more local enterprises would have enormous benefits – from the creation of jobs, to a healthier environment, to a more equitable distribution of resources. Depending on the local situation, transport money could be spent on building bike paths, foot paths, paths for animal transport, boat and shipping facilities, or rail service. Even in the highly industrialised world, where dependence on centralising infrastructures is deeply entrenched, a move in this direction can be made. In Amsterdam, for example, steps are being taken to ban cars from the city's centre, thus allowing sidewalks to be widened and more bicycle lanes to be built.

Large-scale energy installations are also today heavily subsidised, particularly in the South. Phasing out these multi-billion dollar investments while offering real support for locally available, renewable energy supplies would result in lower pollution levels, reduced pressure on wilderness areas and oceans, and less dependence on dwindling petroleum supplies and dangerous nuclear technologies. It would also help to keep money from leaking out of local economies.

Agricultural subsidies now favour large-scale industrial agro-businesses. Subsidies include not only direct payments to farmers, but funding for research and education in biotechnology and chemical and energy intensive agriculture. Urbanised consumers may not be aware that most agricultural subsidies – as well as most of what they spend for food – benefit corporations and middlemen, not small farmers. Shifting expenditure towards subsidies that encourage smaller-scale, diversified agriculture would help small family farmers and rural economies while promoting biodiversity, healthier soils and fresher food.

Government expenditures for highway-building often promote the growth of super-stores and shopping malls. Spending money instead to build or improve spaces for small-scale public markets – such as those that were once found in virtually every European town and village – would enable local merchants and artisans with limited capital to sell their wares. This would enliven town centres and reduce pollution and fossil fuel use. Similarly, support for farmers' markets would help to revitalise both cities and the agricultural economy of the surrounding regions, while reducing the money spent to process, package, transport and advertise food.

Television and other mass media have been the recipients of massive subsidies in the form of research and development, infrastructure development, educational training, and other direct and indirect support. They are now rapidly homogenising diverse traditions around the world. Shifting support towards building facilities for local entertainment – from music and drama to dances and festivals – would offer a healthy alternative.

Economic localisation

Economic localisation, as an alternative to globalisation, means an adaptation to cultural and biological diversity; therefore no single 'blueprint' could be appropriate everywhere. The range of possibilities for community initiatives is as diverse as the locations in which they can take place. Yet one of the effects that they all share is to ensure that the benefit of economic activity is retained in the local community.

Local initiatives cannot be imposed from above, they have to grow from below. However, central government can both deliberately encourage and act to remove the inhibitions to their growth. The following examples are by no means exhaustive, but illustrate some of the steps already being taken.

In a number of places, community banks and loan funds have been set up, thereby increasing the capital available to local residents and businesses and allowing people to invest in their neighbours and their community, rather than in distant corporations.

'Buy local' campaigns help local businesses survive even when pitted against heavily subsidised corporate competitors. These campaigns not only help keep money from 'leaking' out of the local economy, but also help educate people about the hidden costs – to the environment and to the community – of purchasing cheaper but distantly produced products.

Local currencies and Local Exchange Trading Systems (LETS) range from alternative notes to large-scale barter systems. They are an effective way of guaranteeing that money stays within the local economy. Ithaca, New York, is home to one of the more successful local currencies, called Ithaca HOURS. Begun in 1991, the system has over $50,000 of local currency in circulation today, and is used by over 1000 participants. Other currencies based on this model are already being used in 12 states in the United States.

In operating a LETS, people list the services or goods they have to offer and the amount they expect in return. Their account is credited for goods or services they provide to other LETS members, and they can use those credits to purchase goods or services from anyone else in the system. Thus, even people with little or no 'real' money can participate in and benefit from their local economy. LETS schemes have sprung up in the United Kingdom (where there are over 250 in operation), Ireland, Canada, France, Argentina, the United States, Australia and New Zealand. They have been particularly beneficial in areas with high unemployment. In Birmingham, where unemployment hovers at 20 per cent, the city council has been a co-sponsor of a highly successful LETS scheme. These initiatives have psychological benefits that are just as important as the economic benefits: a large number of people who were once merely 'unemployed' – and therefore 'useless' – are becoming valued for their skills and knowledge.

A further type of initiative is the Community Supported Agriculture (CSA) movement in which consumers in towns and cities link up directly with a nearby farmer. In some cases, consumers purchase an entire season's produce in advance, sharing the risk with the farmer. In others, shares of the harvest are purchased in monthly or quarterly instalments. Consumers usually have a chance to visit the farm where their food is grown, and in some cases their help on the farm is welcomed. While small farmers linked to the industrial system continue to fail every year at an alarming rate, CSAs are allowing small-scale diversified farms to thrive in growing numbers. CSAs have spread rapidly throughout Europe, North America, Australia and Japan. In the United States, the number of CSAs has climbed from only two in 1986 to 200 in 1992, and is closer to 1000 today.

The prospects for the good life

Despite such initiatives, the globalising style of economic development that the world is pursuing is moving us all further from the good life. However, this is not an inevitable process – and there are alternatives.

Yet economic localisation is very far from being the normal pattern of development. How realistic is it to expect this pattern of development to prevail?

The obstacles are formidable. One of the consequences of economic globalisation is that the relative power of individuals and small businesses declines. This decline is both in terms of economic power but also now increasingly in political terms and in social significance generally. This means that the effective resistance to localisation will increase over time.

Yet it is easy to be pessimistic. A first, and permanent, step is to acknowledge that there are quite different forms of economic development from the one which is separating us from the good life ☉

Helena Norberg-Hodge is an anthropologist and and author of Ancient Futures: learning from Ladakh *(Sierra Book Club, 1991).*

Adrian Henriques is Manager of Social Audit Practice at the New Economics Foundation.

Against the addictive society

The good life depends on balance and integration but much of modern life encourages addiction and compulsiveness. **Helen Wilkinson** calls for a recovery programme for the addictive society.

> *Compulsiveness is for us one of the prime enemies of the good life... The problem for all of us today is to establish relatively stable lifestyle habits which, however, don't slip too far into compulsiveness... I believe we do now live in a society scarred by compulsiveness. The furthering of individual autonomy and self-esteem in everyday life should be regarded as just as important a political task as legal and other freedoms in the public sphere.*
>
> Anthony Giddens, *Conversations with Anthony Giddens*

In the West, we seek the good life, but, we have created an addictive culture which takes us further away from it. We glorify and celebrate this culture, while simultaneously turning a blind eye to its negative effects. This attitude plays out in almost every sphere of our life. And until we resolve this central contradiction, our search for the good life will remain ever more elusive.

Consider our attitude to alcohol. As a society, we love alcohol. Traditional rites of passage from adolescence into adulthood are celebrated in pubs and bars. The ritual continues at college where binge drinking is almost de rigeur. For many people, this pattern continues in their adult life. For others, it slows down, but still we associate alcohol with the good life: red wine and cheese after dinner, a quick gin and tonic to unwind after work – alcohol is intimately associated with our leisure and our pleasure.

But here's the rub. When the problems of an alcoholic culture come home to roost, we grow judgemental and scornful. Attitudes to alcoholics and alcoholism have scarcely changed in 150 years. Alcoholics are stigmatised, cast out as 'the other' of our culture, never one of us. So when we see the winos on our streets we shake our heads at people who don't know how to handle their drinking and who lack the self-restraint that divides the alcoholic from the rest of us. Some of us might feel pity, sad that they must hide their problems behind drink, but ultimately we feel safe, unchallenged, because they are not one of us. And precisely because our culture has created a sense of shame concerning alcoholism, we ignore or turn a blind eye to the problem drinking that is all around us – whether it's our own, our lovers, our friends and family, our co-workers. We go into denial because the dominant message in consumer culture is that alcohol is richly satisfying, part of our life, as essential to the good life as summer holidays.

Alcoholism is one of the more obvious addictions, but there are others and, precisely because they are less obvious, their effects are more pernicious. Let's take our attitudes to work. Any balanced notion of the good life would suggest that we should work to live, but instead we seem to have created a culture where more of us live to work. The Protestant work ethic trades on this notion of work as morally redeeming to the soul. It tells us that work is good. As does New Labour. In this context, it is not hard to see how we have created a culture in which work is all important as a source of self-identity to more and more people. Every day, in subtle and insidious ways, we glorify and celebrate a workaholic culture. We reward 'presenteeism' and many of us look down at those who leave work on time, assuming they lack commitment. We even test our co-workers on their capacity to handle stress, letting the demands and pressures mount to see if they really can take it.

Our attitudes to those who fall by the wayside are in themselves revealing – the people who opt out of the linear career, who refuse to play the game – are written out of corporate history, as failures, B-graders rather than high fliers. We pity the victims of early heart attacks and feel embarassed around those who have suffered nervous breakdowns, privately dismissing them as failures, or somehow weak. We blame the individuals, rather than the cultures that they have fallen foul of. Only rarely do we ask whether a work culture that puts people under such unhealthy pressures is sustainable, or indeed desirable.

Alcoholism and workaholism are some of the better known addictions. But there are many more. In America, the country which prides itself on excess, almost any form of indulgent (or self-denying) behaviour now comes with a label. The list is endless: there are drug addicts, chocaholics, shopaholics, leisureholics, email addicts, exercise bulimics as well as regular run-of-the-mill bulimics. And as a society we are also addicted to a celebrity culture both as onlookers and as insiders. Princess Diana paid a heavy price for her own media addiction (and ours). Politics too can become like a drug: the power, the media and the status are a quick fix.

Clearly some addictions are more serious than others: retail therapy seems small fry if it keeps you from indulging a serious cocaine addiction. But the key point is this: the range and scope of unhealthy and dysfunctional behaviours seems to be growing. And the good life seems ever more elusive. With its litany of excess and addictions, it's hardly surprising that America is in the vanguard of experimenting with solutions. The therapy culture so skilfully satirised by Woody Allen is its natural offshoot, as is its confessional culture. Having a therapist is part of the lifestyle package, as are confessions to almost total strangers. In places like New York, or San Francisco, almost everyone you meet owns up to having one or more addictions within the first five minutes (most are relatively harmless). And many readily admit to having, or wanting a therapist. This is a great contrast to Britain, which is still to a large extent ensnared in a 'shame culture'. The confessional spirit is inhibited, although it is beginning to gain a voice.

The therapy culture is not without its dangers and therapy can itself become as psychologically addictive as any other activity or drug (perhaps we should label it therapy addiction). And as any therapist will tell you, people who have buried and denied feelings for so long, invariably go through an equally vulnerable (and somewhat tedious) phase of 'confessionalism'. Having opened the floodgates to our emotions, we suddenly indiscriminately confess our feelings to almost anyone: how we hate our boss, feel hurt by the mother in law or want to kill the new born baby. The public reaction to Princess Diana's death had some of this quality. It is as if once our guard has been dropped in the safety of the therapist's room, we retreat to a state of childlike innocence. Rather like Humpty Dumpty having fallen off the wall, we suddenly find ourselves having to find the fragments of ourselves and put them back again. This is not just an ad hoc, stop/start kind of process, it is also a somewhat volatile one. Emotionalism and confessionalism is all well and good in the safety of the therapist's room, but in the wrong hands such confessions can leave us unprotected, and vulnerable. (This is a pattern that can itself create another reason for therapy. And so the cycle goes on, as does the client's embryonic therapy addiction.)

There is a danger that the therapeutic process can feed this child-like dependence as the individual signs over power (and responsibil-ity) to the therapist and ultimately the whole process runs the risk of replacing a shame culture with a blame culture. The answer it seems is to encourage the individual to 'own' their own recovery, rather than simply relying on professionals. Hence the growth of 'recovery' culture. Alcoholics Anonymous, having started as a meeting between a few alcoholics in one house, has become a worldwide movement, and has since spawned various off-shoots: Narcotics Anonymous, Overeaters Anonymous, Bulimics Anonymous, Workaholics Anonymous and Artists Anonymous (for blocked artists and cre-atives). This recovery culture is pervasive. I was made aware of this within weeks of arriving in New York last Autumn, when I came across an article quoting Barry Manilow, describing himself as a 'recovering celebrity'.

For the addictive personality, the challenge is to switch from unhealthy addictions to healthier ones – from prozac to St John's wort, from a bottle of scotch or a bottle of wine to a bottle of orange juice, from a box of chocolates, to a bar of chocolate to no chocolate. But the road to recovery is a long and tortuous one and the process can become addictive itself. As one man in recovery said to me, 'I don't want to spend as much time in self-help groups as I spent drinking and drugging'. He has a point.

These caveats aside, for many struggling individuals, therapy and self-help groups are clearly part of the answer. Countless individuals have begun to take personal responsibility for the predicaments that they find themselves in. This may be a route to their own salvation, but as a social solution, such self-help programmes fall short. For ultimately, they deal with effects, not cause. They involve taking remedial action when a problem or an addiction has become unmanageable, but they don't stop it developing in the first place. For the reality is that, what-ever one's actual addiction or vice, whether it's alcoholism, worka-holism or some other holism, the culture that condones it is the root cause of the problem. So if we are to tackle the causes, as well as the consequences of our own addictions, we need to look at the addictive culture we have created for ourselves. Then, collectively, we need to take steps to recover from it.

How might this be done? What role can and should politicians play? What recovery programme can and should a government take to change the culture which sustains addictive and dysfunctional behaviour? The first step is surely to recognise that the key to 'the good life' lies in *balance* and *integration*, in all facets of our lives – between our personal and professional lives, between our working life and our family life, between our material lives and our spiritual lives.

The second is to recognise that this lack of balance distorts our perspective on life, and sets us up to adopt dysfunctional patterns of behaviour: the way we love, the way we work, the way we use drink or drugs. The third is to identify the 'holic' pressures which promote an addictive culture. The fourth is to introduce policies such as parental leave, flexible working, which promote balance and integration, and which minimise the desire for the quick fix (that bottle of wine to unwind after a hard day at the office, that pill to allay your anxieties).

The fifth step involves recognising that, for some, it is the tyranny of too much rather than too little time, which is debilitating. As is well-documented, the experience of unemployment and underemployment fuels a sense of isolation, depression and disconnection which can in turn foster an unhealthy dependence on addictive sub-cultures. Government can and should take steps to foster a sense of self-worth among less advantaged groups, by providing meaningful work promoting debate on what we mean by worthwhile work. For example, if we gave greater public recognition of the value of informal caring in our communities and in our families, we could begin to shift the culture away from its unhealthy obsession with paid employment as the source of all meaning.

The sixth step, and one of the most important, involves us all recognising that the boundaries between our private lives and our public lives, the personal and the political, are being redrawn, and that if politicians are to moralise and preach about the good life, they must walk the talk. In this sense, the government should conduct an audit of its own addictive subcultures, such as the culture of workaholism which pervades Westminster and Whitehall. By modernising the working hours of the House of Commons and Ministerial departments, the government could set the tone for a healthier workplace culture for the nation as a whole. But they must also educate through personal example.

Of course, disembedding the cultures of addiction we have created can only occur over the long run, and governments can only do so much. One day at a time, one step at a time ... but the political 'recovery programme' must go on. For although the addictive culture seems glamourous and seductive, it is ultimately dysfunctional. It sets up a vision of the good life that is compelling to many of us, only to take it away. It promises the quick fix, the immediate high, but it cannot sustain it. It sets up a fantasy life which falls far short of the authentic good life. And while as individuals we can confront the corrosive effects of this culture in our personal lives, it is ultimately to politics and politicians that we must turn if we are truly to create a crisis of legitimacy around the addictive cultures we have as a society created ☉

Helen Wilkinson is Project Director at Demos. She is currently on sabbatical in California, enjoying the good life.

© *Helen Wilkinson 1998*

Shop while they watch

The information age promises a wealth of new goods, services and home comforts. **Neil Barrett** warns that the virtual good life will have its dark side.

This is the 'information age', in which the economy depends on the exploitation of information. Global computer networks such as the Internet make an unimaginably vast amount of data available at almost zero cost. On-line publications, Usenet news groups, personal and corporate homepages – all these and more ensure that we have as much information as we can ever hope to obtain on every imaginable (and many unimaginable) subject. The information age, though, spreads wider than simply computer networks: GSM telephony means we can stay in touch wherever we might be, from the top of Mount Everest to a supermarket car park in Swindon; digital television brings the promise of hundreds of channels, catering to every conceivable interest group; and data processing devices are embedded in everything from motor cars to cash cards, from washing machines to CCTV.

The 'digital good life'? To an extent, perhaps, yes. The technology of the information age certainly makes huge numbers of modern devices ever more efficient. It helps to support people in working from home. It even allows those people to carry out their work from more attractive, rural locations, if that's what they wish. And of course, the technology provides facilities for what we might call 'informational self-sufficiency': with such a wealth of raw information sources to hand, individuals need not be dependent upon establishment sources for their news, political coverage or indeed anything else. For those with the wit to take advantage of it, the global information pool of the Internet is a staggeringly powerful resource.

Set against these advantages, however, is a terrifying variety of problems that impact upon our organisations on the one hand, and on our-selves as individuals, citizens and consumers on the other.

Looking first at organisations, the digital good life does indeed seem to be an appropriate term for the operating environment within most offices. Computer resources make the whole range of commercial tasks far easier, from the trivial aspects of typing letters to the complex elements of managing a 'just in time' distribution system. Organisations, attracted by the promise of enhanced profitability, have pursued more and ever more computerisation – but at what cost?

Initially, the first organisations to embrace information technology were able to outperform their closest rivals. But increasingly, as rivals themselves have moved to using computers, investment in IT is essential no longer simply for staying ahead of the pack, but for keeping up with it. And this dependency translates into a vulnerability: a computerised organisation whose computers fail no longer drops back into the pack of competitors; instead, the organisation drops further behind them. Indeed, in many cases those organisations whose computers fail – whether from a terrorist bomb, as in London a few years ago, or from sabotage, fire or simple system failure – routinely and inevitably go bankrupt. The panic about the looming 'millennium bug', serves as the starkest reminder of this vulnerability, even if the panic itself proves ultimately to be unwarranted.

If the growing dependence on the tools and toys of the digital good life is worrying for organisations, it is surely even more so for individual citizens. There is a wealth of information available throughout the global conglomeration of computers, databases and networks that serve the consumer economy that we enjoy. But what sort of information do those resources include?

Consider a typical working day. At 7am, the radio alarm bursts into life. You stagger to the kitchen, putting lights on, setting the coffee pot to boil; you take a shower and you dry your hair with the electric hairdryer. Your electricity requirements have leapt from near zero to a working level, your water likewise. This use of electricity and water is all metered, and the first series of datum points about you – a specific individual – is collected and recorded in a variety of databases.

Perhaps you use the washing machine. The computer chip in the control unit records the type of wash and the date and time you turned it on. You make your way to the office, driving your car past three, four, perhaps even more traffic-monitoring cameras – another datum point.

You stop to fill your petrol tank, paying with your debit card. The time, the location and the amount are recorded. But this gives more than one simple datum point about where and when you stopped. It provides a coherent record of how far you routinely drive, and it shows information about your regular routes to and from work, to your family and so forth. And if you make a series of calls from your mobile phone, in addition to whom you called and for how long, your location, your direction of travel and even your speed can be deduced from the operator's records.

A clear picture of your behaviour as a consumer is being steadily constructed.

You arrive at the office. Perhaps you have a swipe card to check in; the time is recorded. Maybe you make a series of telephone calls; the time, the destination and the duration all are recorded. Your work may involve trawling the Internet for information; the sites you visit are recorded. The 'click-routes' you took through those sites are analysed and – on that basis – highly customised advertisements are presented to you. At lunch-time, you go to the supermarket, using your loyalty card and a debit card to pay for the weekly groceries. Your preferences are noted and analysed; any non-standard purchases can be examined and assessed. Perhaps you buy extra toilet paper over and above your regular requirements (plausible deduction: you have a guest staying with you). Perhaps you buy a video or a magazine (the content can be analysed, and what it says about you can be understood).

Throughout any day, any individual leaves behind them a snail's trail of data, a series of personal information snapshots that can be analysed to build a clear and coherent picture about who they are, what they do, what they like, how they think. In the information age, you have precious little privacy. The virtual good life generates new discontents: our IT-based conveniences can only be used at the risk of unprecedented personal 'transparency' (see Perri 6's article in this *Collection*).

The saving grace, of course, is that these information resources are all separate and uncoordinated. Some of the databases – supermarket purchasing histories, banking and telephone records – are especially powerful, and others would be so if they could be combined and 'data mined' to produce a more comprehensive picture. Moreover, elements of privacy are afforded under the terms of the Data Protection Act of 1984 – legislation which is due to be brought up to date. Under this Act, data collections on such personal information must be gathered, maintained and manipulated according to a set of clear conditions. Where data collections are unfairly aggregated, are incorrect or have been collected in an unlawful manner, the subject to whom the data relates has a clear and obvious recourse to the law.

Unfortunately, it is not quite as simple as that. Two aspects of modern life combine to confuse the issue. The first is the location of many of these databases – particularly those that result from Internet activity. The majority of Internet host servers are located in the United States, a country having no data protection rules and therefore subject only to self-imposed restrictions on data use. This is a problem, but not an insurmountable one: data protection laws throughout Europe are now emphasising the question of controlling the export of data to those countries not supporting 'adequate' controls.

The other aspect of modern life that is perhaps more worrying in this context is what we might call the 'personal information economy'. Our economy is increasingly dependent on the trading and exploitation of information – and much of that information is personal data. And in many cases, the subjects themselves conspire in their own exploitation. Loyalty cards, club membership details, Internet activity, purchasing preferences: all of these have been knowingly made available by subjects in return for services, giving potentially global visibility of themselves and inviting everything from junk mail to nuisance callers. And that data can be mined and analysed in ever more sophisticated ways to construct the most comprehensive picture of the individual's life.

The price of the personal information economy is therefore simply this: universal visibility not just of what we buy or do, but of who we are and how we think. We might be on the verge of living the digital good life, but if so, we will live it in a digital glasshouse ⊙

Neil Barrett is a Fellow and Consultant on IT security at Bull Information Systems. He is the author of The State of the Cybernation *(Kogan Page, 1997).*

© *Neil Barrett 1998*

The gene genie

Caroline Daniel asks what the prospect of genetic self-enhancement will do to our pursuit of happiness for ourselves and our children.

Hugh and Sarah Bennett wanted the best for their children. Don't all parents? They had both worked hard in their careers, and had been putting money aside into a special bank account for a number of years now. They called it their 'gene bank'. It was easy enough to get their child listed at several of the major public schools, but nowadays that didn't seem enough. Indeed, the costly education could even be wasted on a child if they weren't genetically predisposed to be intelligent.

No. Why gamble on a genetic lottery when you could at least fix the odds a little. Surely it was right to make sure that their child would grow up to be physically attractive, a certain skin colour, tall, with blue 20/20 vision eyes and a slim build. For a bit more money the Bennetts planned to insert some extra intelligence enhancing genes, which they had heard could boost memory, or some genes to improve musicality. Sure, the efficacy was hard to prove. But it was worth it. They knew their investment would benefit not just their kids but their grand-children. It was a real investment for the future – a genetic legacy.

This is just one vision of enhancement: germline gene therapy. This involves reprogramming germline cells (sperm or egg cells) and so alter the generic makeup of unborn descendants. A second vision of enhancement relates to improvements to individuals that cannot be handed on to future generations: somatic gene therapy. It involves the correction of genetic defects in any cell in the body (other than repro-ductive cells). As the human genome project unravels more genetic codes for particular features, both physical and behavioural, the pos-sibilities of enhancement are seemingly endless, from inserting a gene to prevent hereditary baldness, or changing one's weight, to incorporating genes from different species into human DNA.

These possibilities are already moving from science fiction to fact in animal research. Already researchers are sprinkling extra genes into animal DNA to turn them into superior beasts. Cows have been engineered to beef up their beef. Scientists at the Roslin Institute in Scotland created Dolly the sheep, a 'transgenic' lamb genetically tweaked with an extra human gene so that it produces Factor IX, a protein which plays a major role in blood clotting. The firm hopes to be able to milk (literally) Polly for this drug, which is expensive to produce by other means. And the Cambridge firm, Imutran, has added human genes to pigs, to try to make them suitable donors for human organ transplantation. All these experiments suggest that human genetic makeovers will be possible one day.

Some potential moral teething problems are already being addressed, too. In America, people are already trying to improve their kid's genes. People can select sperm over the Internet, taken from men with a high IQ, a certain skin colour, an athletic build and even a taste for Indian cuisine. In September, doctors at a Virginia fertility clinic said they had developed a system that allows couples to choose the sex of their babies, using a sperm-sorting machine designed for animal breeders. The technique does not guarantee a sex, but tilts the odds in favour of a particular sex. The process is now available for family balancing (to adjust the boy-girl ratio within families). As such techniques become common, it's not such a great moral leap to allowing parents to select a few other features they would like in their child. Opinion polls suggest that if people could improve the intelligence levels or physical characteristics of their children through genetic therapy, a majority of Americans, and a smaller number of Brits, would do so.

More generally, there is already interest from individuals seeking to enhance themselves. In America, requests have come in from patients who have heard about genetic developments. One patient, learning that genes for skin pigment had been identified, asked his doctor if he could help him change his skin colour. A sports medicine doctor heard that genetic therapy was being designed for muscle diseases and wanted to know if he could get access to the treatment to help healthy athletes grow bigger muscles.

For now, gene therapy has proved extraordinarily unsuccessful. And germline therapy remains a rare taboo in the genetic field. But it will not always be so. So should we worry about genetic enhancement? Is better always good?

The first question is what exactly is genetic enhancement? Some people have tried to answer this by drawing neat demarcation lines between 'negative' and 'positive' uses of gene therapy. Typically, genetic modification to enhance human ability beyond its normal limits is seen as negative, whilst treating genetic diseases is seen as positive.

In practice this neat rule breaks down. Drawing a clear line between enhancement and treatment is difficult. Technology originally intended to treat a serious disease may prove to have cosmetic uses too. Just as Prozac has caused psychiatrists and doctors to rethink the boundaries of what is a 'normal' mental state, and to prescribe the drug for ever more conditions, so gene therapy will impose new questions about what is 'normal', what kind of weight, skin colour and so on are acceptable. Even if research into genetic enhancement was banned, there are likely to be any number of serendipitous side-effects from research into genetic treatments.

Take weight control. In 1994, scientists identified a gene in mice, the ob gene, that appears to have a big influence on obesity. Mice without the gene were unable to regulate their appetite control. But when mice were injected with the ob protein they experienced a 30 per cent weight loss. When this protein was injected into mice with normal ob genes, they too lost weight. Obese individuals would clearly be interested in this potential treatment. But so too would those who want to be thinner for cosmetic reasons. Whose responsibility is it to decide who should be able to have access to this technology and determine the boundaries of treatment and enhancement? On what basis could people be prevented from taking advantage of this form of therapy?

The first line of defence are issues of safety and efficacy. The risk–benefit ratio will be hard to assess. How could we tell whether the insertion of an extra 'gene for intelligence' was effective if it was introduced into an embryo? It would to impossible to compare the resulting child with one who had not had the extra gene sprinkled into his DNA. It may be many years before it is possible to find out if any of the enhancement had actually worked – just as it may take years for potential downsides to be truly understood.

The very idea of enhancement is subjective. For example, the US Food and Drug Administration, when it was making a decision about how to regulate liposuction devices, concluded that the best way to characterise the benefits was in terms of 'patient satisfaction'. Traditionally, agencies require less proof of safety and efficacy for cosmetic treatments. One individual may decide the risks of genetic manipulation to create green eyes outweighs the hassle of contact lenses, which have the same effect. Others may feel differently.

While some of these decisions about risk are for individuals to ponder, there are larger issues at stake. Genetic enhancement may be good for individuals but not for society. Genetic enhancement is unlikely to be available to everyone. The primary roadblock will be cost. Prenatal and germline therapy will involve expensive techniques such as IVF, which are not available to all. Enhancement through somatic gene therapy will be costly and, like cosmetic surgery, unlikely to be available through the public health system or most private insurance schemes. So only the rich will be able to take advantage of these new techniques. Genetic advantage could combine with pre-existing economic advantage. Theoretically at least, this accumulation of advantage could have serious consequences for our notion of equality of opportunity.

More prosaically, there is the potential for cheating. There are likely to be forms of genetic therapy to enhance someone's muscular build that could be especially valuable for athletes. Would it be fair to compete against these people in sports contests? And, given that the gene which makes muscles grow occurs naturally in the body, how would it be possible to detect those who had enhanced themselves?

Again, context matters. It is hard to say all forms of genetic enhancement will have terrible effects on society. Would William Hague really want to pass a law to ban genetic therapy to cure hereditary baldness? As for the question of access to advantage, society has not really made tremendous efforts to ensure that everyone has equal access to other sources of advantage like public schools, or cosmetic surgery, so why should access to genetic enhancement be so different?

So, while a blanket ban on genetic enhancement does not make sense, there is still a need for lifeguards to safeguard the gene pool, to police forms of genetic enhancement that could pose serious risks to equality. If genetic enhancement does become sophisticated enough to enable people to alter their skin colour, or massively boost their IQ, or rid people of the plagues of ageing, then we are talking about much more serious issues of inequity ⊙

Caroline Daniel is a writer and journalist with the New Statesman.

Part 3
Strategies for well-being

Timeless values

Despite massive progress in material conditions, modern societies have gained little insight into the deep questions about how we should live. **Geoff Mulgan** calls for renewed attention to fundamental sources of well-being.

Is life getting better? It is notoriously hard to say. By some measures, the progress of societies in the twentieth century has been extraordinarily fast. We are less than one lifetime away from the Great Depression, the gulags and the holocaust. In the early 1930s, Gandhi understandably said, in answer to the King of England's question, 'What do you think of Western civilisation?', that it would be a good idea. At that time, Europe's quarrelling nations still presided over vast empires, many of them held together by vicious oppression. Most of the world's population lived in abject poverty, most women had few if any rights, and racism was the norm.

A case could be made that little progress has been achieved. During the past 50 years, the world's climate has begun to show the strain of coping with humanity and worse acts of genocide have been committed, from Europe to Cambodia, than ever before. A widespread response, not least among intellectuals, to the dark side of the last century has been to conclude that civilisation has not advanced and that progress is an illusion.

But if this reaction is understandable it is also partial. By staggering contrast with the human predicament during the 1930s and 1940s, most of us in the West live in peace, the empires have crumbled, democracy has become mainstream and huge opportunities have opened up for millions of people who, a generation ago, would have had little choice about how to live their life. Our lives, in the West at least, are on average longer, healthier, freer and better informed than our ancestors'. Despite the prevalence of absolute poverty, the same is true for many millions in the developing world.

So if most of us in the West have the chance to lead far more prosperous and comfortable lives than any generation in history, what of our *capacity to live them well*? Here the picture is far less rosy. Despite the explosion of magazines and manuals on how to live, and the new industries of therapy, counselling and relationship advice, it is hard to find much evidence of progress in our understanding of how we should live, of what constitutes a good life. The ideas of philosophers and prophets from more than 2,000 years ago – Buddha, Jesus, Confucius, Lao Tse – have, remarkably, not been superseded. Indeed they still speak to us with clarity and persuasiveness where their contemporaries' ideas about science have become curiosities.

This paradox – massive progress and change in the facts of life, combined with surprisingly little progress in our understanding of the qualities of the good life – is one of the oddities of the millennium, a rare moment when the world has a chance to take stock of what has been achieved, and of what it wants to take into a new era.

What lies behind the paradox? Perhaps the answer lies in the nature of modernity. The world around us has been shaped, more than anything else, by the pursuit of happiness in a just society, for heaven on earth rather than in the afterlife. Each of its elements cannot be understood except in these terms: the spread of democracy widening the circle sharing in the fruits of economic growth; the spread of a capitalist market fuelled by material aspiration; the migration of millions to the Americas in search of a place to thrive.

In the case of people brought up to accept grinding poverty and disease as the natural order of things, this hunger for a better life needs little explanation. Yet its effect was to blind the prophets of modernity to the question of how we should live. Great attention was paid to *processes* – the procedures of democracy, the rule of law, the mechanisms of the market. But only the dissenters troubled themselves with questions about the *purposes and outcomes* of institutions and individual lives that had been common in ancient Greece: how should we live, how should we manage our desires?

Modernity has now reached a point where this gap in its make-up has become unsustainable; partly because what in the past would have counted as material plenty has become the norm for the majority in much of the world; and partly because the slow retreat of religion that has coincided with the spread of a capitalist economy has left a gaping hole in millions of people's lives.

We need, in short, to find a way of talking honestly and openly about the good life – good both in the sense of being satisfying and being ethically based. But to do so we first need to escape from some of the myths of the good life. The most powerful comes from extreme individualism. A famous philosopher once asked how the same good life could ever be right for a human race composed of people as different as Marilyn Monroe, Einstein, Wittgenstein and Louis Armstrong. Any single view of the good life, he argued, must inevitably be oppressive. The best that we can hope for is a society in which everyone is given as much freedom as possible to define the good life for themselves.

This view is undeniably attractive. It accords with the 'non-judgmental' common sense of most Western societies today. Yet it is as profoundly wrong as any belief could be. Any society which took it seriously would soon become dysfunctional. It is wrong, in the first place, because so much about the good life is not solely a matter of individual freedom, but is underpinned by collective provision, by social orders, by the things we share – clean air, safe streets, civility. It is wrong too because human beings have much in common: we share much the same biology, and many of the same drives and needs, however different we may appear on the surface. And it is wrong because it ignores the evidence that there have been remarkably constant features of the good life across very different times and very different places. However much the good life may appear ephemeral, and however much our lives are radically different from the nasty, brutish and short lives of most of our ancestors, some things are timeless and universal. The same elements go to make up a crucial part of what we understand as a good life.

I find it useful to think of these as *attractors* – common elements that drive and motivate people in otherwise vastly different societies. Five stand out.

The first is the family. Throughout history, the great majority of people have chosen to live in families. They have sometimes been extended, sometimes nuclear, sometimes combining three or more generations, sometimes involving polygamy. But the family unit has provided emotional sustenance and unconditional support far more than any other institution, as well has having practical virtues as a way of sharing resources. Families can be brutal and dysfunctional, as can communities, nations and religions. Yet the family is the most decisive shaper of well-being and happiness, the place where our essential humanity – our capacity to reproduce and to be part of the chain of life – finds its purest expression. For all its radical changes in form in the last generation, the family both as an ideal and as an everyday social unit has proved to be remarkably resilient, remaining, as Christopher Lasch termed it, a 'haven in a heartless world'.

The second is the community. People like to live in society, in contact with friends and acquaintances. Beyond the family, the community provides recognition, meaning, opportunities. Like the family it can at times oppress and divide. But it provides both the order that we need to have a fair chance of thriving – predictability, habits, and protection – and a context within which we can make a good life.

The third is access to goods for sustenance, adornment and play. These have always been attractors, from the earliest trade in amber and shells to computer games. Today's shopping malls play on our attraction to shiny, enticing objects, and consumption can easily turn into addiction. Yet we should always beware of condemning the all too human desire for material things (as Auden warned, 'as a rule it was the pleasure-haters who became unjust').

The fourth is the environment. The good life depends on good air, water, trees and landscapes. People have made lives in an extraordinary range of environments. In each they have found a way to live with an ecosystem, and become acutely dependent on its twists and turns. Our dependence on the environment is crystallised in the religions that turn it into deities, and it is now being reintegrated into our understanding of the good life.

The fifth is the soul: the spiritual dimension to life has often existed in tension with the ties of family and community, and the lure of physical things. But a spiritual understanding of transcendence, of connectedness, and awe in face of the universe, has been made manifest in the church, temple or mosque at the heart of every community. While other attractors are about complexity, filling up our lives with meanings and possessions, this deep element in the good life is about simplicity and fundamentals. As the mediaeval Christian mystic Meister Eckhart commented, God is not found in the soul by adding anything but by a process of *subtraction*.

What lessons do we draw from the timelessness of these five attractors? As individuals, we know that good lives have been made out of these materials, as well as out of our luck, and our genes. From them we construct shapes, meanings, challenges, resolutions, that together make up a biography and, ultimately we hope, a pattern. From them, and from reflecting on them, we make a life (indeed this is the heart of ethics: as Socrates argued, an unexamined life is not worthy of living).

Yet it is a peculiarity of modern Western political thought that it has so little to say about these attractors. Marxism tried to deny the need for all five (and in some societies Marxists achieved some 'success' in obliterating not only the family, community and the environment, but also religion and material provision). Liberalism has often been suspicious of the pull of these archaic ties, and capitalism has for 200 years been attacked for its spiritual hollowness, its squeezing of time and energy out of the family and community and into work and commercialised leisure.

Each system promised the good life, but through a fundamental deception. Communism promised the achievement of human freedom and potential, but asked that these be suspended in the interim. Capitalism, by contrast, as Adam Smith argued eloquently in *The Wealth of Nations*, has always been based on the deceitful nature of an invisible hand that encourages people to work in order to gain essentially worthless things, 'trinkets and baubles' as he put it, that do not make them happy.

In the first flush of early modernity it is not surprising that theorists forgot the enduring lessons of the elements of the good life. But now we have abundant scientific evidence to confirm the foundations of well-being: material plenty, certainly; good health; strong relationships; membership of a religion; recognition.

So what should we do with this knowledge? First, we need to leave behind the terror of judgement that has made being 'judgemental' a cardinal sin in an age of popular sovereignty, multiculturalism and consumer choice. The truth is that we can make some judgements about the goodness of lives: not only their ethical qualities, but also aesthetic ones, how much sense, meaning, coherence they have; how much a life is fulfilled; how much a life leaves a legacy. These judgements will often be contested, and the capacity to make judgements should never again be monopolised by an elite or a priestly caste. But it is not true that all lives are equal, any more than all art is equal. There are enduring distinctions to be drawn between the good and the bad, the excellent and the mediocre. Great works of art can still communicate and still overpower our senses, just as great lives, in all their myriad forms, can still inspire us, and just as good technologies enrich our lives, and stretch our capacities, whereas bad ones leave us docile and unsatisfied.

Second, we need to learn to be at home in the past and in the future. Ever since the industrial revolution, it has become common for progress to be counterposed with reaction, modernity with tradition. But any proper understanding of the good life has to acknowledge both the capacity for progress and the timelessness of many fundamental values. It needs to be open to the benefits of technology, and also to the virtues of a simpler life in which more space is left for meaningful living; open both to the marvels of great buildings and, like the best new urban planners, to the virtues of village-like communities; open both to the value of freedom in relationships and to the enduring values of family attachments. This is not having your cake and eating it; it is, rather, the only sensible response to the paradox of progress.

These are still early days. For many people, any discussion of the good life may seem like a distraction from more pressing problems of poverty and social exclusion. Even in unprecedentedly rich societies experiencing steady growth it can still be easy to push quality of life questions to the margins, to see them as luxurious add-ons, to be thought about when the important fundamentals have been got right.

Carl Jung once said:

> 'all the greatest and most important problems of life are fundamentally insoluble... They can never be solved but only outgrown. This "outgrowing" proves on further investigation to require a new level of consciousness. Some further or wider interest appears on the horizon and through this broadening of outlook the insoluble problem loses its urgency.'

I believe that many of our most acute problems are, in fact, soluble. But the dissatisfaction that many people experience with their lives, and with material plenty, is not one of them. Unlike unemployment, ill-health or inequality, it is a problem waiting to be *outgrown* rather than solved, as our culture moves from the pursuit of growth for its own sake to an understanding that is more familiar in the natural world and in the great religions: that growth involves *deepening* too ⊙

Geoff Mulgan founded Demos in 1993 and was its Director until October 1998. He is an advisor to the Prime Minister and a member of the No 10 Downing Street Policy Unit. This essay is adapted from a lecture given in January 1997.

Private lives

Perri 6 identifies the importance of private life to the good life and argues that strategies for protecting it must involve compromise, given people's conflicting views of privacy.

Private life

No explorer has ever discovered humans who have no system of kinship or community. Yet nearly every society seems to value a space for solitary contemplation. In every society we know, dwellings are arranged to keep at least some of their contents free from the uninvited gaze. If you want to trace it all back to our primate origins, orang-utans are highly solitary, gorillas stick to the family and for much of their time chimpanzees operate in loose bands. We humans, meanwhile, appear to want a compromise, being by turns 'groupish' and solitary.[1]

Western ideas of privacy and private life are not obvious things for many of the world's citizens to aspire to. When, in the mid-1980s, I found myself staying in a hamlet in the remote semi-desert of Tunisia, the idea that I might want a few minutes to myself, even that I might prefer not to be observed while defecating, was regarded as strange, and slightly insulting to my hosts' hospitality. On the other hand, if there is any truth in the old tale about late nineteenth century Australian aborigines objecting to being photographed, I suspect that it may have had little to do with being deprived of any spiritual substance, and rather more to do with the intrusiveness of personal information being collected without consent. Yet codes of practice on respecting privacy have not been a major priority either in agrarian north Africa or in hunter-gatherer societies.

Only in the twentieth century did private life become something that the mass of Europeans could hope for, when formerly aristocratic ideas

[1] Ridley M, 1996, *The Origins of Virtue*, Penguin, Harmondsworth.

of dividing the rooms of a house for separate functions and for individuals to have their particular room became common (even nobles only acquired the habit in the eighteenth century).[2] The physical separation of household space appears to provide a powerful domestic analogy for the galloping rate at which the division of labour has separated different spheres of life in modern times.[3] This has in turn rendered individuals much less dependent upon their kin and neighbours than were people in mediaeval times. As soon as private life became socially possible and available, people seem to have welcomed its benefits – perhaps something of the orang-utan shows through the skin of the chimpanzee here.

The idea of a distinct arena of public life is as modern as that of a private life.[4] Indeed, mediaeval life had few public institutions or spaces for public life either in the sense that ancient Romans and Greeks understood public life, or in any modern sense. Private life and the public sphere are products of the same fundamental change.

However, since the Enlightenment there has been a growing conflict within our conception of the good life between the claims of the public and private spheres. Indeed, the defining battles of our politics have often been framed in these terms – liberalism stands for the return of religion to the private sphere, Jacobinism and many later extreme sects stand for the subjection of all private life to the public scrutiny of the movement, and so on. Since the 1970s, most European and north American societies have sought to regulate this conflict ever more carefully with legislation such as data protection laws, laws governing media intrusion and laws specifying police powers.[5]

The private

Added to this there are conflicts about what areas the 'private' actually covers:

- *private people* are those who do not hold public office
- *private organisations* are those that are not state owned
- *private facts or activities* are those that are known only to a small number of people
- *private issues or behaviour* are those that are not a legitimate matter of scrutiny by authorised others
- *private places* are those to which access may legitimately be denied to others

2 Perrot M, ed, 1990, *A history of private life, volume IV: from the fires of revolution to the Great War*, tr. Goldhammer A, Belknap Press of the Harvard University press, Cambridge, Massachusetts; Prost A and Vincent G, eds, 1991, *A History of Private Life, Volume V: Riddles of identity in modern times*, Belknap Press of the Harvard University press, Cambridge, Massachusetts.

3 Schoeman FD, 1992, *Privacy and Social Freedom*, Cambridge University Press, Cambridge.

4 Habermas J, 1989 [1962], *The Structural Transformation of the Public Sphere: An inquiry into a category of bourgeois society*, Polity Press, Cambridge.

5 Bennett CJ, 1992, *Regulating Privacy: Data protection and public policy in Europe and the United States*, Cornell University Press, Ithaca, New York.

Perri 6

6 See Boling P, 1996,
*Privacy and the politics
of intimate life*, Cornell
University Press, Ithaca,
New York. See also
Weintraub J, 1997,
'The theory and politics
of the public/private
distinction' in Weintraub
J and Kumar K, eds,
1997, *Public and pri-
vate in thought and
practice: perspectives
on a grand dichotomy*,
University of Chicago
press, Chicago, 1-42.

- *private property* is that which is subject to largely unrestricted personal property rights
- *private interests* are those of specific individuals, groups, organisations, industries or identities.[6]

Different people value some of these areas over others. For example, many feminists value the economic role of private property, but consider that the risks of domestic violence and abuse of children in the home are such that privacy should not protect everyday home life from

Figure 1. Rival conceptions of what is valued in private life and privacy protection

Grid

Social relations conceived as if principally involuntary

Fatalists

Systems are capricious
Private life is a residue of discrete elements after surveillance and accountability have brought much of life into the social domain

Privacy is not particularly valued

Civic republicans

Systems are necessary
Private life is a sphere of retreat, preparation and paedagogy in which civic virtue is inculcated

Privacy is valued in its place, but with qualifications and balances

Individual autonomy should not always be held accountable

Individual autonomy should be held accountable

Liberals

Regulated systems are superfluous or harmful
Private life consists in a limited set of legitimate rights to control the use of personal information about oneself; this control can be traded in exchange for other services by rational individuals

Privacy is valued, but can be traded

Egalitarians

Systems are oppressive except when they protect
Private life is an unjustifiable claim to a protected sphere, and in practice protected from public accountability behaviour that is often unacceptable

Privacy is only valued instrumentally to protect egalitarian movements against unsympathetic authority

Social relations conceived as if principally involuntary

Private life as discreet experiences (individual)

Private life as a sphere (especially family)

scrutiny. Free market liberals value the institution of private property and consider it threatened by the lobbying activities of private interests upon the state.

Traditions and cultures

In a recent book,[7] I suggested that one way to understand these different sets of values is to work with two basic ideas that seem to be found in every human society: the idea of choice and the idea of accountability. If we categorise people firstly according to the degree to which they believe that all social relations should be modelled upon voluntarily chosen ones, and secondly the degree to which they believe that individuals should be accountable for their own choices, then we can distinguish four basic perspectives on private life and privacy.

The four main areas describe quite different preferences that people have for privacy. While surveys have often suggested that most people are willing pragmatically to trade privacy for other benefits, it is far from clear that many high street consumers are impressed with service enhancements they are offered in exchange for permitting more data to be collected about them. Certainly, it is becoming evident from recent research that simply offering benefits does not mean that even pragmatic consumers are prepared to forget about privacy concerns.[8]

The rise, fracture and conflict of liberalisms

The rise of privacy is the story of liberal law-making. Breach of confidence first became a tort in English law when in 1849 Prince Albert sued to prevent a Mr Strange working in partnership with a Mr Judge from exhibiting and distributing copies of private etchings made by the royal couple for their private use, Strange and Judge having procured them from the royal printer. The judge (lower case) who heard the case remarked that the prince should have his injunction not only on the grounds that his property had been seized unlawfully but also that 'the privacy and seclusion of thoughts and sentiments' deserved protection. On these words a shaky body of law has been erected which has been used against the press and many others for violations of privacy.[9] However, privacy law did not develop greatly until the 1890s when, in that most liberal of countries, the United States, lawyers Warren and Brandeis wrote an article arguing for a specific tort to combat the invasions of the yellow press. In those days of innocence, the worst excesses of journalists were thought to be the gatecrashing

7 See 6 P, 1998a, The Future of Privacy, Volume 1: Private life and public policy, Demos, London.
8 6 P, 1998b, The Future of Privacy, Volume 2: Public trust in the use of private information, Demos, London.
9 Wacks R, 1989, Personal Information: Privacy and the law, Oxford University press, Oxford: 82ff.

of private house parties. Data protection laws arrived much later, in the 1970s, when the computer became the principal means by which personal information is stored, manipulated, matched with other information, mined to create profiles and to collect the evidential basis for decision-making by credit rating agencies, public authorities administering taxes and benefits, the police and others. These legal developments are the footprints of a the rise of a liberal individualism increasingly in conflict with the economic liberalism that tends to reinforce the power of commercial organisations to use personal information freely.

The personal information age
The new information society is not simply a matter of the power of information technologies. In that sense, the advent of writing and then of printing have made all civilisations into information societies, and computing represents only an incremental change. What is genuinely new is the power of organisations to collect and manipulate personal information on an industrial scale, and the emergence of an economy for which personal information is the basic fuel. Data capture through smart cards, data warehousing and the buying and selling of databases are not merely additional strategies for competitive strategy by firms: they are the heart of the new capitalism. And the consumer trust issues for businesses, which vary in importance according to the extent to which organisations commit themselves to information ethics, are increasingly central to the conflicts between individuals and organisations. At the heart of these conflicts is a competition between an *economic* liberalism of business freedom to dispose freely on intellectual property and a *political* liberalism that asserts the rights of individuals as consumers or citizens to have some control over how information about them is used.[10]

Viability
In some measure, then, the experience of private life is probably an integral element of anything we would recognise as a conception of the good life. But no complex society agrees about what exactly is valuable in private life, or what exactly should be protected in the name of legitimate privacy. The four or five basic cultures that find themselves in disagreement wax and wane at different historical rates. How then can we think about the role of public policy in a field like this,

10 For a detailed discussion of the scope and meaning of privacy in the context of media law and ethics, see 6 P, 1998a (note 7).

where there are profound disagreements about a key element of the good life, and where any settlement will necessarily exceed the bounds of the legitimate for some, and fall short for others?

While economic textbooks of public policy would begin with cost-benefit analysis, or some other formal procedure in which some utilitarian calculus is embedded, the analysis of cultures and traditions I have offered here suggest that, on the contrary, *the important point of policy is conflict management*. Indeed, the essence of a civil society is its ability to manage the social and ideological conflicts that arise from the political articulation of competing cultural impulses in a civil manner. In other words, a society that is restrained, willing to accept compromise, avoids winner-takes-all politics and accepts that virtues are plural.[11]

A useful tool for understanding how the competing cultural views of privacy can be settled through conflict management is that of *cultural viability*. Cultural viability tests the robustness of strategies of conflict management by asking which strategies are most effective across the widest range of plausible settlements between the conflicting views. It also asks what strategies are least vulnerable to the shocks that might arise from cultural views that have been excluded from any settlement.

There is not space here to set out the details of culturally viable strategies for data protection policy, journalistic powers of investigation, genetic information and insurance, and so on.[12] However, it is important to recognise that a concern with privacy, which has been so clearly buttressed by the experience of private life since the 1800s and by reaction against the scale of dataveillance that underpins modern business and capitalism, will not simply die out of our culture in the face of the growing power of data matching, mining and warehousing methods. On the contrary, the new consumerist ethos is actually reinforcing the importance of information ethics for many people. Nothing so central to business and government as personal information can be expected to become a triviality in complex and culturally conflict-ridden societies like those of North America and western Europe. It is a foolish misconception of technological determinists that processing power alone will force culture to 'adapt' by people resigning themselves to the abandonment of important, hard-won and recent values that are reasonable responses to the experience of modern living itself. No privacy policy that is built around such an assumption can be culturally viable.

11 Shils E, 1997, *The Virtue of Civility: Selected essays on liberalism, tradition and civil society*, ed Grosby S, Liberty Fund, Indianapolis.
12 For detailed arguments and recommendations on these points, see 6 P, 1998a (note 7).

Good life, private life and viable life

If this general argument is right, then it has great consequences for how we need to think about the good life and the role of public policy in supporting its possibility.

First, our conception of the good life must recognise the importance of people's desire for private life. But it must also recognise that we do not and cannot all agree on what it is that we *value* in private life. Therefore, the good private life is inevitably a compromised affair – but, crucially, one in which a compromise is reached that is genuinely civil and culturally viable. That compromise may be more biased toward the protection of privacy than some economic liberals, extreme egalitarians and extreme civil republicans might like.

Second, and more broadly, any conception of the good life in general must be at once pluralistic and accepting of civil compromise. Human lives are too much involved with each other for any us to be able to realise our own conception of the good life without affecting others, or for any idea of 'neutrality' of the state and society between conceptions of the good life to be achieved or culturally viable. For example, privacy, whatever each of us values in it, is not achieved in private, but in social peace. Conflict management is therefore at the heart of any social practice that can sustain good lives.

Third, the best strategy for enabling people in culturally conflict-ridden societies to live good lives is to pursue strategies that are culturally viable, given what is known about the plausible patterns of cultural dynamics and the making and breaking of settlements between cultures.

Whatever bounds biology may set upon our ideas of the good life and the things we might value in privacy, it is civil compromise and cultural viability that make the experience and practice of groupish and solitary life genuinely 'good' in both the moral sense and in the sense of practical desirability. Such conclusions do not please ideologues or those who consider economic reasoning or technological development to be the sole criteria on which viability or desirability of social arrangements is to be founded. But they offer the richest and most developed idea of civil life that I know of. In short, the good life for the many is the viable life for the most ☉

Perri 6 is Director of Policy and Research at Demos.

Juggling the good life

Geraldine Bedell

In 1989, an ailing women's glossy magazine was relaunched as 'the magazine for women who juggle their lives'. *She* was a grown-up *Cosmopolitan* for the me-generation mother who wanted babies, career, sex and designer shoes. In 1995, the editor of *She*, Linda Kelsey, resigned, pleading stress and the wish to see more of her small son. The magazine quietly removed its 'juggling' cover lines and it became an established truism that while it may be possible to have it all, it's not possible all at once. The vision of having it all as endless bountiful consumption was over.

But the dream won't go away. We are still groping towards having it all, if in a slightly different version; and for very good reasons. Sixty-four per cent of mothers are now in the workforce. There is widespread unease over the state of masculinity: men are somehow meant to be heroic, sexy and, at the same time, empathetic, communicative and handy with a duster. Beneath the debate over whether Viagra and Xenical should be available on the NHS lies uncertainty, both about our entitlement to happiness and how cheaply it may be bought. And the popularity of self-help books – *Men Are From Mars, Women Are From Venus* and *The Little Book of Calm* – reveals a similar reaching for the quick-fix, the direct route to the complete lifestyle.

Having it all, in fact, has become an even more onerous vision of the good life than when it was coined to describe women who merely had children and careers. The revived enthusiasm for mutuality threatens to impose a further set of obligations on the individual, this time to the community. And then there is the need for lifetime learning, or its New Ageist equivalent, personal growth. Looking at the range of responsibilities to self and others entailed in having it all, the enterprise looks doomed from the start.

Which is not necessarily to invalidate it as an ideal. There are two ways of looking at how individuals might increasingly move towards their own, custom-tailored version of having it all. The first is to think in terms of what one might call the negative good life – in other words, what obstacles need to be removed to enable people to make the least-constrained personal choices. The notion of having it all must look absurd, even insulting, to anyone living in poverty or to full-time carers with no respite. But even for people not in this plight, there remain structural constraints on choices – there is still no national childcare strategy, no statutory parental leave and, for all its fine talk, the government's interest in parenthood, as exemplified by the Child Support Agency, doesn't seem to extend much beyond the paying of bills.

There are workplace constraints, too – although there is the chance that the growing apprehension of workers as brains or skills for hire could help to remove such barriers and glass ceilings as still exist for women. Increasingly flexible employment arrangements and flatter structures inside companies could allow individuals to move in and out of employment without these harming their careers. Greater life expectancy and improved health ought to enable individuals to work into their fifties, sixties and even seventies, perhaps to pay back debts incurred in their child-rearing years.

Maximum flexibility is the ideal, since the balance between work, family, volunteering and self-fulfilment will differ between individuals and at different stages of life. (Fiftysomethings are the boom sector for long-distance adventure travel; people in their eighties are more likely to focus their attentions on family and community.) But removing the constraints on making these choices, and enabling them to be revised, is not the end of the story.

The second approach is to consider the cultural context in which the choices are made. That the having it all ideal exists at all is testimony to the plethora of options on offer. We are restless in our affluence because we know that around the corner is always some other absorbing opportunity – to be the perfect parent, the successful business person, the valued member of any one of a number of communities, whether local, vocational or familial. It's no wonder that the self-help books concentrate on finding a space among these clamouring demands to reflect upon who one is.

In the 1980s, the response to this cornucopia was an Ab-Fab-style consumerism which, in practice, was only available to the rich, successful and extremely energetic. Now we seem to be evolving towards a more mundane but widespread and inclusive notion of balance. Even as we pursue everything today, we expect to be thwarted; having it all has become a euphemism for not going all-out for any one thing. It's about compromising and settling; it involves an acceptance of limits and a degree of renunciation.

While a little anxiety over the conflicting pulls of self-realisation and responsibility may well be a useful prophylactic against smugness, renunciation doesn't have to mean misery. It all depends why the sacrifices are being made; a lot hangs on the quality of the resulting relationships.

The early, me-me versions of having it all offered no convincing account of how or why one might do without. Communitarianism, with its pious emphasis on sacrifice for the community (which so often leaves one feeling that somehow women will end up doing the sacrificing), seems too hair-shirt to be attractive. But at last, we seem to be evolving towards a more positive understanding of renunciation, not only as something that one occasionally does for the greater good (using the car less for the sake of the environment), but also as something worth doing for oneself.

Home and family, for men and women alike, have become more legitimate preoccupations. It is no longer unacceptable to talk about one's children as a prelude to a business meeting; it is more acceptable to leave the office for a school concert than for a dash round Harvey Nicholls. Meanwhile, a recent Meryl Streep movie, *One True Thing*, shows Hollywood shifting its focus from unmarried women and working girls on to the domesticated female, an object of scorn or neglect for at least two decades. Daphne Merkin, the *New Yorker* film critic, has written that 'something lifts the movie above its [weepie] genre – something that points to one of those cultural shifts that films, almost unbeknownst to them, occasionally foreshadow.' The shift is not – or one certainly hopes not – the glorification of the full-time mother, but the recognition that complex, energetic people are not axiomatically selfish, and can be found doing all sorts of things.

There is, admittedly, still some way to go. Neo-Conservative commentators have deplored the loss of Victorian values that once lent legitimacy and status to family devotion and economic improvement alike. Myron Magnet lists these as 'deferral of gratification, sobriety, thrift, dogged industry and so on, through the whole catalogue of antique-sounding bourgeois values'. It is true that they sound not only antique, but also dreary – although, on closer examination, they may have quite a lot to recommend them. Certainly, individuality, boldness, enterprise and innovation, while all admirable, carry their own contradictions, undermining as they do tradition and attachments.

So in our efforts to reconcile the contradictory pulls of autonomy and responsibility, which is largely what having it all is all about, it seems that we need to find a new nexus of values that ratifies the pleasures and rewards we derive from both self-realisation and self-denial. It will be much easier to have it all if we can recognise how much pleasure, as well as virtue, there is in muddle ⊙

Geraldine Bedell is a novelist and journalist with Express Newspapers.

Small is bountiful

Nicholas Mellor explores the links between work and well-being – and discovers that small enterprises can lead us to fulfilling lives.

Will there be such a thing as a safe job in the next millennium – for anyone? The future is ever less predictable, with the shift towards a totally globalised economy and its complex interdependencies. Emerging technologies are changing the way we do things in all walks of life. The consumer society encourages a defensive reaction – to put our faith in what we can acquire directly – immediate, guaranteed gratification. It is easier to focus on simple tangible gains, and to respond to or accept the events around us. The scale of the economic and social forces at work is bewildering, and we, as individuals, tend to become reactive to our environment rather than proactive. These sweeping changes and institutionalised frameworks that regulate society often distract us from considering what is going on at the individual level, and taking responsibility as individuals for helping shift our lives towards greater well-being.

As we approach the turn of the century, there is a pervasive feeling of losing control, and an awareness that our overly self-centred lifestyles and our focus on material values not only fail to make us happy but are the prime culprits for the cracks in the cohesion and environmental sustainability of our society. Searching for support from external structures, whether from organisations for which we work, or from legislation aimed at ensuring a minimum level of welfare for all, turns out to be less rewarding than we may have hoped.

When working in a large organisation we need to conform to its structures, its processes. Like a termite colony we can become very efficient at what we do, but the appropriateness of such a high level of adaptation and loss of individual initiative is thrown into question by a rapidly changing environment. What could be described as a finely tuned, highly structured organisation – such as a termite colony – could also be seen as a case of evolutionary stagnation.

For three years I worked in a large pharmaceuticals company developing new medical products. Some of the products – such as the first genetically engineered vaccine – were of enormous significance, with a gestation period longer than the length of the career with the company enjoyed by most people involved working on the project. An individual could only make a difference to a relatively small element in the total project. The compensation for being a small cog was a clear hierarchy and a set of corporate values that helped shape my aspirations and helped map out a route for achieving them. The complication was that the route reflected how things had been in the past, not how they were likely to be in the future. I was defined more by what I did than who I was, and what I did was a small part of the complex work of a very impressive termite mound.

Since those days I have been involved with a number of start-up organisations, both in the voluntary and commercial sectors. Some have failed, some succeeded. It has been a rocky ride, but involvement with small enterprises has radically changed my perspective on strategies for survival, and the nature of personal fulfilment. The scope for learning, evolving and making a contribution is far more attainable in a network of small, diverse and interdependent bodies, where the variety of habitats is likely to provide a greater variety of means through which an individual can contribute, than within large organisations.

Working as part of a small organisation has many advantages in the development of a better quality of life. At the simplest level there is the fulfilment that comes from the ability to make a difference more directly, over a shorter time frame. One can see the consequences of one's actions more clearly, whether in terms of the business, the community or the people in the organisation. That gives you a greater opportunity to learn, to adapt, and to reflect on the coherence between your own values and the values that drive the organisation.

The scale of the organisation is directly related to its ethical dimension and the quality of the relationships which develop: *the smaller you are the more you need to collaborate to survive.* Any relationships tend to be based more on trust than power. Being small you are often inherently outward looking and therefore more likely to value diversity.

You are more aware of the tensions and imbalances in dealing with the conflicts that arise from limited resources and time. Not every dilemma has a clear-cut 'right' solution and we need to live with the decision we make. There is no chance to put to one side the ambiguity of many decisions – to rely on an external code of conduct, or precedents that may have be set in larger or longer lived organisation.

Making the most from limited resources means constantly seeking to work at the margin where the most significant difference can be made in adding value. For a humanitarian organisation it means reaching out to where the need is greatest – where if it was not for their action, there would be no help. For a research-based company it is to take those ideas that would not otherwise be realised and to make them happen, to turn them into real products and services. In a start-up organisation there is no *status quo* that we can fall back on.

It leads to a perspective where you are more aware how interdependent we truly are, and the extent to which we need to put our trust in a network of relationships, with colleagues, suppliers, customers or beneficiaries. You are more aware of the value of mutual support. As Lord Young of Dartington wrote in his foreword to the Demos report on 'Employee Mutuals'[1], mutual aid is still the kernel of society, in the tradition of David Hume and Prince Kropotkin. The interdependencies recognised and celebrated in the traditions of mutualism are rarely more evident that in a start-up organisation. We depend on what we can contribute today and in the future and the speed with which we can build up that network of trusted relationships. Fulfilment is largely linked to our sense of self-worth – the extent to which we are recognised both in our personal and work relationships. It is directly related to how others see us, and the belief that we are able to contribute to society, and enhance the quality of life for other people.

To make that contribution we need to be proactive. We need to be aware of our scope for contributing. We need the imagination to see how we might make a positive difference, the importance of which has been so well described by Beryl Markham: 'I learned what every dreaming child needs to know – that no horizon is so far you cannot get above it or beyond it.' The new ventures in which I have been involved have taught me that you are unlikely to get there in a single step, but that the effort can open up inspiring vistas.

We need to be given the chance to do make this kind of contribution within the framework of mutual enterprise, the independent will

1 Leadbeater C and Martin S, 1998, *The Employee Mutual: combining flexibility with security in the new world of work*, Demos/Reed, London.

to see it through and the conscience to learn from it. And if it fails we need the support of others in a joint enterprise to try again. Learning to take such initiative is a crucial element of the true good life. Andrei Sakharov, an indefatigable dissident and inspirational moral force in Russia under the Soviet system, quoted the preface of Goethe's *Faust* in his *Reflections*: 'Of freedom and life he is only deserving who every-day must conquer them anew' ⊙

Nicholas Mellor has been involved in setting up MERLIN (Medical Emergency Relief International), Datamark Ltd and the Life Sciences Network. He has worked in industry and as a management consultant.

Good business

Charles Handy argues that capitalism and growth must be rethought if we are to use them to promote individual and collective well-being.

The next century may well be heralded as the Age of Autonomy in the Western societies. It may not be all good news if it turns out that way. We are, as Sartre said, increasingly 'condemned to be free', free of institutions, free of imposed accountabilities, free of imposed obligations to others. We are all, more than ever before, on our own. This applies to businesses as much as it does to individuals, leaving us all with the uncomfortable question to resolve for ourselves - 'what is it all for - our life and our work?' The recent interest in the moral basis of society may well be an expression of an intuitive worry about what will hold us all together, now that we are so free.

Individualism, both in our own lives and in our businesses, is one of the basic freedoms given to us by democracy and capitalism, a combination which has been heralded as 'the end of history' in the sense that there is nowhere else to go in a search for progress. Yet, as Francis Fukuyama, pointed out in his book of that name, it will not be unadulterated bliss. The combination may, in fact, result, he says, in our lying down like dogs in the sun, wanting to be fed and tickled by those whom we elect, who know that they will not be elected if they do not promise us our desires.

Capitalism has turned out to be seductive. It has proved immeasurably better at delivering the goods than any other system. It has, however, yet to prove that it can also deliver a good life for all, or a decent society. It has been our mistake to assume that, on its own, it could ever do that. Capitalism is a mechanism not a purpose for life. The means, however efficient, cannot be used to justify whatever ends happen to result. We need to keep this horse of ours in harness, not roaming free, in order that we may go where we want to go. Which, once again, begs the great philosophical question - what is it that we are aiming for? It is a question which may have no conclusive answer but it must, nevertheless, be addressed if we are not to drift, indifferent or indignant, into the next century.

We used to belong somewhere. To families most obviously, but also, most of we males anyway, to a work organisation. These two communities were the bastions of our lives, hate them or love them we belonged to them. Families still thrive, and some 75 per cent of people live in a household with two adults at its head, although those households are not all as they once were. One 15 year old vividly and proudly described her family in a recent interview:

'I've got two mums and two dads, lots of brothers and sisters, and none of them are actually whole. they're all halfs and steps and bits and bobs and I love them.... If they're talking about love from your family I suppose you should have as many parents as physically possible.... Everyone whom you consider family is family. Friends can be family.'

It sounds free and fun but these families are now, like the labour market, more flexible than they ever used to be, where flexibility is, however, a euphemism for uncertain. If it isn't working, don't fix it, seems to be the new message, just leave. Avoid commitment, feel free to jump when opportunity knocks and free to leave when it stops knocking.

The same is true of organisations, once the other central institution in our lives. The government has in the past proudly brandished surveys which show that 83 per cent of workers are 'permanent' although, on investigation, permanent appears to mean a little less than 6 years, which is the average length of an employment contract these days. Only 35 per cent of the workforce have been with their current employer for more than ten years, and over 50 per cent are, at best, loosely linked to one, being part-time (25 per cent), self-employed (13 per cent), temporary (8 per cent) or unemployed (7 per cent). Perhaps the survey asked respondents if they were 'permanently part-time' to which the answer might truthfully be 'I hope so!', but a wish is not a truth, nor can you simultaneously boast of Europe's most flexible labour market and of permanence in employment. We are all mercenaries now, on hire to the highest bidder and kept there as long as, and only a long as, we are worthy of our hire or can't find a higher bidder.

Businesses, themselves, are also becoming more autonomous. To be sure they have to keep a watchful eye on their shareholders, must continually delight their customers on whom they depend, and take proper care of their employees and their suppliers and any other stakeholders, but every sensible business does this, and as long as it does it, it is effectively, free to do what it likes. International businesses are particularly independent. There are 70 corporations bigger than Cuba, all of them, like Cuba, centrally-planned economies, often with a dictator of sorts at their head. Owing duties to all the countries in which they operate they are, in their totality, responsible to no one country. As long as their investors are happy, and customers queuing up, they are free to determine their own future.

Where all is so uncertain, where commitment is risky and institutions are interested only in their own survival, selfishness has to be the prevailing ethic.[1] Dog must eat dog and devil take the hindmost. Where freedom reigns, equality disappears. It is not a pleasant prospect. If we want any taste of the good life we have to re-invent capitalism, to restructure its institutions and give it a nobler purpose.

Reinventing capitalism

The combination of self-interest and altruism can be a powerful one. Business is best placed to demonstrate that the two can be combined, best placed to show how wealth can benefit all, best placed, too, to create some of the social capital which many feel is eroding fast, as a direct consequence of our new freedoms, best placed, too, to build institutions that make it seem worthwhile again to belong to something bigger than ourselves. To business will fall the task of redeeming capitalism, to demonstrate that it can indeed work to the good of all, not just the fortunate few, that the creation of wealth can be a glorious thing.

The first task is to recognise that a business can no longer with any justification be called the property of its owners, who are more correctly called its financiers. When the majority of the assets of today's businesses are those so-called 'intangibles' - their people, it must be more realistic to think of a business as a community not a property. A community belongs to no-one, people belong to communities. You cannot buy, sell or merge communities without the consent of its members, its citizens. The recognition of the citizen corporation will

1 See also Sennett R, 1998, *The Corrosion of Character: The personal consequences of work in the new capitalism,* Norton, London.

dramatically change the power balance, reducing the role of the financiers to that of mortgage holders who may continue to trade their mortgages in the market but cannot sell the underlying assets, the business, unless the business has defaulted.

Citizen corporations are more likely to win the commitment of their citizens, more likely to look for a purpose beyond their own survival and growth, more likely to put the quality of the lives of their citizens into the efficiency equation because those citizens will have some civil rights in the corporation. Profit will remain essential, but it will be increasingly accepted that it is a means to an end, not an end in itself. If you focus too hard on the bottom line, it was said, you may sink to it. Successful businesses already know that they need to have a larger purpose. Few people other than the major shareholders are going to jump out of bed in the morning enthused with the idea of 'increasing shareholder value'. They want something more to justify a life, more even than the means of paying for their own daily bread. They don't need grandiose visions of conquest or market dominance, they want declarations of why they exist, for others.

The second need, therefore, is to anchor the business community in its surrounding social community. Propinquity reminds us of our proper priorities. If the ultimate purpose of business is to help build a more prosperous and better world then it should start at its own doorstep, not be delegated to some remote centre or discharged by writing a cheque for tax. Global thinking is supposed to work hand in hand with local action, but this needs to be reinforced by such things as more local responsibility, more local taxation; more local accountability in the governance structure and more direct involvement by its citizens in the local community. If people can see the fruits of their business activity transforming their bit of the world before their eyes they are more likely to believe that their business really does have a purpose beyond itself.

The reinvention of capitalism demands the radical changes outlined above: a new deal for the members of each business as a community and a new focus on the linkages of the company in its local community. But these transformations will not be enough. A new ethos for capitalism must also involve a reinvention of our ideas about growth and the good life, as argued by other authors in this Collection. How should we understand growth and its relationship to our well-being?

The paradox of growth

If more people are going to have enough of the good things of life there has to be growth in the economy. Those who dream of a zero growth society are blinding themselves to the practical consequences. Stagnant ponds stink. Money is sticky, left to itself. It doesn't spread, it clings. Without growth, the available wealth would tend to collect in ugly little clusters, creating ghettos of rich and poor. We need the momentum of growth to keep the stuff moving, to give opportunity to those without it to get their hands on some, without having to grab it from those who have it.

The paradox is that while growth creates opportunity, growth is often fuelled by envy. Production is propelled by the desires of the consumers. When we have all we need, growth would falter unless we moved on to what we want but do not necessarily need, and we tend to want what others have but we do not. This starts to breed an economy of useless things, what the Japanese call chindogu - little umbrellas on your spectacles to shield them from the rain, electrically warmed toilet seats, mops on the bottom of your slippers to polish the floor as you walk, and so on and so on. Christmas is rapidly becoming the chindogu festival.

More seriously, perhaps, an economy fuelled by envy creates a society doomed to dissatisfaction, a society where very few will experience the 'feel-good factor', because there will always be things which others have which they would covet, where the 'positional goods', the things valued for their scarcity value, will always, by definition, be less than the demand for them. If a club is valued for its exclusivity, it loses its cachet if it opens its doors to all who want to come, therefore it remains exclusive, leaving all those outside envious and unhappy.

You could argue that those with money have a duty to spend most of it to boost growth, but if, by doing so, they only magnify the envy of others, and set themselves on a road which has no ending, because there is always more to make or more to buy, then is it worth it? A society dedicated to growth can become a society enslaved by its own desires and discontents, but a society without growth is probably a society where endeavour and experiment are no longer worth the aggro, a society, therefore, without a future. Paradoxes like this have no easy resolution; they have to be lived with, not solved. A judicious balancing of the opposites is the only way to go. Three thoughts may help with the balancing.

The doctrine of enough

The first step to personal freedom is a definition of 'enough', enough money, enough things, enough promotion at work, enough professional renown. If you don't know what 'enough' is, then you will always want more and, by definition, will never be satisfied, or free to do anything else, because you can never know the meaning of 'more than enough'. I have friends whose pursuit of ever higher achievements in their work is impressive, whether they define achievement in monetary terms or in influence and fame, but I see, too, that they are enslaved by the chase. They have no time or energy for anything else, and when the chase perforce is ended for them, often by early retirement or redundancy, they are left without cause or momentum, their life has been used up. If that chase of theirs is some noble cause or vocation, then one can but praise their dedication and their sacrifice, but if the chase is mostly to satisfy personal wants then the sacrifice has to be questioned. For it is a sacrifice of the opportunity to be or do something other. Those who are poor out of choice are the ones who are no-ones slaves. We each of us, therefore, need to work out what is our acceptable level of poverty, our personal definition of 'enough', if we want to make the most of our life.

An upper limit to 'enough', in our own interests, must be balanced by a lower limit, for others. If 'more than enough' is unnecessary, 'less than enough' is intolerable, and should be recognised as such by a decent society. Balancing the two definitions of enough, the upper and the lower, would keep growth going but spread the stuff around in a more equitable manner.

Doing not making

It is fashionable to say that we ought, as a society, to be making more things, to increase our manufacturing. Fortunately, as I see it, we are increasingly concentrating on doing, that is on services. Of course, we need to make things in order to reduce our dependence on other societies for the necessary goods of living, and to have something to sell, but too many things do clutter up the world and steal from its resources. Looking after people, teaching them, keeping them fit and healthy, providing them with housing, help and information - these things can only add to the quality of life without detracting from the quality of the world around us. The growth sectors in all modern economies are now in education, health, caring, personal and information services.

The one thing, I believe, that you can never have 'enough' of is betterment - better health, better education, better quality of life, better contributions to the world around. There is, therefore, no real limit that I can see to the beneficial expansion of these 'good for you' services, provided that they do not become another form of consumerism. My friend who is on a different and ever more extreme diet each month is not an easy guest. For her, diets have become a consumer good, cunningly disguised as a search for betterment. We have to be careful that the chindogu philosophy does not spread over into the betterment area. As long, however, as we are on our guard in this respect, we can encourage growth in this part of the service sector without creating a world of envy, because there is no reason why everyone should not be more healthy, know more or be better cared for. It is not a zero sum game, but one where everyone wins.

Minimising money

Rather perversely, making money the measure of all things restricts growth, because it forces one to price inputs and outputs and to compare the two. The more the outputs exceed the inputs the more 'efficient' the activity is deemed to be. Efficiency then becomes the goal, not effectiveness. You can run a more 'efficient' hospital by limiting the types of admissions and then tailoring your inputs accordingly, a more 'efficient' railway by concentrating on the most used routes, and a more 'efficient' school by practising a rigorous selection process. By pricing everything, the money economy perceptibly grows, while the actual level of activity declines, because fewer people get to travel or go to hospital and fewer people are needed to work there.

If either the inputs or the outputs remain unpriced, real work can grow more easily. Most voluntary organisations would have to close if they were required by law to pay all their workers a minimum wage. Because the work of those that continued would then get counted in the formal economy, there would appear to be economic growth even though lots of people were losing out. If people had to pay cash for all their health care at the point of delivery the demand for treatment would fall dramatically. The more, therefore, we can make services free at the point of delivery the more they will be used, the more people will be needed to work them and the more the real economy will grow. When Rowland Hill reduced the price of a letter to a uniform rate of a penny (almost free), the volume of mail increased dramatically, as did the literacy level of the population and the resulting economic activity. The ultimate effectiveness greatly outweighed the initial inefficiency. Similarly, the more work that can be gifted, as it is in the home, for instance, as well as in the voluntary world, the lower we can price the outputs and the more they will be used.

Rediscovering the soul

Plato maintained that the soul had three parts, a desiring part, a reasoning part and 'thymos' or self-worth. I suspect that, in large sections of modern society, desiring (or consuming) and reasoning (or efficiency) have dwarfed the element of self-worth, which comes in large part from a sense of making a difference, from a feeling of responsibility for others and from the satisfaction of living a life that is not a lie, one that is true to our real values. This is as true of businesses as it is of individuals.

If we want to restore the soul to our society we really need to rethink our economics and to adopt the doctrine of 'Enough'. Paradoxically the end result would not be less growth, but more growth and, I believe, better growth because more widely shared ⊙

Charles Handy is the author of many books on organisational change and the future of work and enterprise. His latest book, The Hungry Spirit, *explores the ideas presented here in more detail.*

© *Charles Handy 1998*

Trade fair

Can we learn to consume sustainably and ethically?
Simon Zadek argues that we need to consume less
and in new ways so that the world's poor can have a
better deal.

Consumption is what we do every day. Yet even the most dedicated shopper knows that something is wrong, as we replace our kitchens, upgrade our cars, get stuck into one more tub of imported ice-cream and exotic beer, and jet-away on another Caribbean holiday. Bettering-the-Jones's is neither good for our physical health nor for our relationships with each other, let alone the environment. And then there is that awkward matter of all the people not invited to the party – over a billion impoverished *under*-consumers.

Yet we keep consuming, encouraged by the conviction that it is the core expression of our power of choice and self-expression. We are even persuaded that we are moral as consumers, oiling through consumption the economic machinery on which we rely for our livelihoods. After all, we are often reminded, if we did not produce more polluting cars together with the roads on which to drive them, where would our economy be?

These messages come to us courtesy of a global advertising industry spending £270 billion annually, and governments without the vision or sense to tell the economic emperor that he is stark naked.

Consumption clearly *does* have a darker side, and this is the side revealed by the recently published *Human Development Report* for 1998.[1] Since its launch in 1990, the HDR has come to symbolise the best of both constructive critique and radical pragmatism. It offers us both the most thought-provoking statistics about the way we have organised the world to benefit some and not others, and then profiles people's actions and policy options which together offer a pragmatic and more humane

1 United Nations, 1998, *Human Development Report*, UN, New York.

alternative. Above, all it stresses that the quality of life cannot be measured by financial data, and economic growth alone will not deliver basic needs for all and environmental security.

The HDR describes in vivid detail the underbelly of a global economy driven by a staggering £15 trillion's worth of consumption annually, a doubling in just 25 short years. This consumption has been underpinned by a mushrooming in the use of natural resources, and in the levels of waste and emissions, including a quintupling of fossil fuel use since 1950 and a doubling of use of fresh water since 1960. As the ecologist and businessman Paul Hawken notes in describing the US economy, 'For every 100 pounds of product we manufacture ...we create at least 3,200 pounds of waste'.[2]

The HDR also reminds us that our hedonistic post-war party has not been shared by all. Over a billion people are deprived of basic needs. The world's 225 richest individuals have a combined wealth of over $1 trillion, equal to the annual income of the world's poorest 47 per cent – 2.5 billion people. A further 100 million people in the industrial world are relatively impoverished. A new poverty index for industrialised countries is published this year, which places the UK eighteenth out of 21 countries, with among the OECD's highest rates of adult functional illiteracy and poor health.

We are all used to hearing amazing statistics, but surely this must boggle the mind of the most well-worn consumer of data. Not to take it seriously requires us to be nihilists, hedonists, technological over-optimists – or possibly some bizarre combination of all three.

But consumption is not all bad. After all, we need food to live and a roof over our heads and clothes to wear. Also, those small pleasures of life – that particular food, or ornament – can contribute to reasonable needs that go beyond material subsistence. What we need to understand is how to strike the right balance between the extremes of anti-consumption and the irresponsibility of allowing market signals to define our future.

Indeed, citizens acting as consumers can even do the cause of sustainable development some good. Drawing on a report contributed by the New Economics Foundation, *Purchasing Power: Civil action for sustainable consumption*, the HDR highlights many examples of responsible consumption.[3] In the UK, for example, the fairly traded coffee, Cafédirect, has captured several per cent of the British market, and has encouraged companies such as Nestlé to reconsider the basis of their

2 Hawken P, 1997, 'Natural Capitalism', *Mother Jones Reprints*, San Francisco.

3 Zadek S, Lingayah S and Murphy S, 1998, *Purchasing Power: Civil action for sustainable consumption*, New Economics Foundation, London.

own brand reputations and strategies. Initiatives noted in the report aimed at promoting fair trade and empowering local communities in developing countries – for example, the Global Action Plan and local currency schemes – can localise and moderate consumption patterns by deepening and enriching community-based markets.

In the UK alone, for example, some 340,000 people are involved in purchasing goods that have been fairly traded from communities in the South. Overall, annual fair trade is now worth £350 million. Similarly, 300,000 people in the UK invest their money in 'ethical funds', whose investment criteria are based on an assessment of the ethical and environmental dimension of companies and sectors. This figure is growing annually by 10 per cent.[4]

Added to this are the more challenging civil actions that pressure companies to behave more ethically in their treatment of people and the planet. A significant and growing proportion of the consuming public are willing to take social and ethical performance into account in deciding what to, and what not to, purchase. NEF's report offers numerous examples of this, such as the long-running international Baby Milk campaign, as well as the more engaged Ethical Trading Initiative which is supported by the UK Government.[5]

Ethical consumption is not 'just a rich person's game', as some claim. Women in South Africa have converted their experience at organising consumer boycotts under apartheid to directing purchases towards those companies wishing to invest in social development in the new South Africa.[6] People in shanty towns in Latin America, Africa and Asia have found ways to mobilise to secure that basic services, health, water and electricity are made available.

These community initiatives and demonstrations of solidarity through the market are important, but they seem puny compared to what is needed to bring sanity to the world of consumption. After all, according to the HDR it would cost a staggering £25 billion a year to achieve universal access to all basic services, such as basic education, water and sanitation.

But is this really so much? Europe and the United States spend almost £8 billion annually on perfume, and a stunning £11 billion on pet food. Europeans annually spend £31 billion on cigarettes, and Japanese business runs up an annual entertainment account of £22 billion. And that is all dwarfed by the unbeatable annual bill of £490 billion worldwide on military expenditure. Why is it that these shocking statistics are for-

4 Zadek S, Lingayah S and Forstater M, 1998, *Selling Ethics: Understanding how social labels work*, Report prepared by the New Economics Foundation, European Commission, Brussels.
5 The Right Reverend Simon Barrington-Ward, 1997, 'Putting Babies Before Business', *The Progress of Nations*, UNICEF, New York.
6 Harcourt W and Zadek S (guest editor), 1998, 'Civil Action, Consumption, and Sustainable Development', *Development*, Journal of the Society of International Development, Sage, London.

gotten, shrugged off like water from a duck's back, yet we are expected leap with anxiety or joy when we are told that the economy has grown by 1.25 per cent instead of 1.0 or 1.5 per cent?

We need to consume less and differently for others to consume more, and for future generations to have a fighting chance.

As individuals we have to moderate our excesses and direct our purchasing power to achieve social and environmental 'goods'. These individual actions alone will, however, certainly *not* deliver the priceless good of equitable and environmentally sustainable development. Converting our current unsustainable level of consumption will require the corporate giants that direct our tastebuds, and the governments who should represent our interests, to come forward with products, technologies, laws and tax regimes – and most of all the vision and leadership – that will enable wealthier citizens to act responsibly, and those currently without to consume what they need to live healthily, with dignity, and joy ⊙

Simon Zadek is Development Director at the New Economics Foundation.

Cures for 'affluenza'

Brand names and retail therapy are thriving in our so-called 'post-materialist' culture. **Judy Jones** urges resistance to consumerism using weapons such as subvertisements and junk swaps.

'Switch on the important things in life,' says one of my favourite items of junk mail, from the cable company Videotron: 'money, fame, passion, travel, power, shopping'. An admirably succinct, if somewhat depressing, juxtaposition of the priorities and aspirations of the average citizen as seen by the advertising industry. Such advertising would have chimed with the 'greed is good' ethos that made its mark on Britain in the 1980s, but this perky little mailshot flopped though my letter-box halfway through the supposedly 'sharing, caring' 1990s.

In the post-war years, being a good consumer of mass-produced durables was a badge of patriotism and citizenship. When TV advertising came in during the 1950s, it exploited this synonymity, our instincts to conform with our peers, improve our status, keep up with the neighbours and if possible pip them to some materialistic winning post. Nowadays, however, much advertising increasingly feeds off our fantasies to escape from the hell that is other people, and their boring petit bourgeois acquisitiveness, into some 'inner-directed', more 'natural', post-materialist utopia.

Take cars, for example. No windswept seashore, field of swaying corn or virgin wilderness seems to be complete these days without the presence of a film crew shooting a car advertisement. The message of the advertisement is unmistakable: 'Buy this car, escape from all the nastiness of modern life, all the dreary people you have to share it with, other car users and traffic gridlock, in particular. Commune with nature. Find out who you really are.' Advertising imagery is clearly exploiting a supposed value-shift underpinning the 'less is more' lifestyle trend – a move away from simple consumerism towards a 'post-materialist' set of values and aspirations, as theorised by Ronald Inglehart.[1]

But in doing so, the message becomes ever more absurd: your new pared-down, simpler life is fine, but wouldn't the latest four-wheel-drive make it perfect? Equally ridiculous was the slogan used in a recent campaign for a well-known perfume: 'Just be'. Just be? If that were all we need to do, who would want to go out and waste their money on a bottle of over-priced, over-packaged perfume?

Advertising needs to sell us the same old consumer goods that we don't actually need by dressing them up in new clothes, in perpetuity. Never mind that their production helps to degrade the environment and often reinforces the poverty of developing countries. It keeps big business in the over-developed world in clover, and gives us endless opportunities for 'retail therapy'. But it needs to do that by making us feel good, guilt-free and as ignorant as possible about the costs to the environment and to the developing world; and that the purchase, display and the use of the product is cool, hip, sexy and trendy – generally making us more tolerable and attractive to ourselves and to others.

Can we imagine a scenario for future consumption in which citizens begin to perceive advertising-led consumerism as a treadmill and find new ways to satisfy their wants and needs?

Environmental organisations have achieved a great deal over the past two decades in raising awareness about the need for sustainable production, consumption and development, fair trade and so on. But this awareness is only slowly expressing itself where it counts most, in consumer behaviour. Why? We are saturated with media imagery urging us to buy. Not only are messages about ethical shopping, fair trade and over-consumption but a drop in this ocean of brand advertising, they are often interpreted – if not intended – as negative, admonishing, interfering with personal freedom, promoting a lifestyle of hairshirts and self-denial. In short, they may appear dull, paternalist and pessimistic.

Britain has a fine record in lampooning and satirising the antics of political leaders and their spin doctors, which has encouraged a deep and thoroughly healthy scepticism of the political hard-sell among the voting public. Yet the lunacies and abuses of public communications indulged in by many of the big corporations that create and promote

1 Inglehart R, 1990, *Culture Shift in Advanced Societies*, Princeton University Press, Princeton.

our wasteful, shopaholic consumer culture have largely failed to inspire a corresponding satirical tradition – or at least one that has made any significant headway into the mainstream. Given that some multinational conglomerates are now so large in turnover and global reach that they are capable of exerting more power than many national governments, there has never been a greater need for new forms of cultural resistance and assertion of alternative viewpoints. A popular culture of 'post-materialism' has yet to emerge. Much of the media are either heavily dependent on the revenue that brand advertising brings in, or form simply one arm of a global commercial empire; so perhaps many professional communicators are now reluctant to bite the hand that feeds them, or controls them.

There are some refreshing exceptions. The Vancouver-based anti-consumerism magazine *Adbusters* pulls much the same visual tricks as traditional advertising in order to subvert and satirise it. It is full of 'uncommercials' – spoof ads, spoof ad competitions, stories of 'culture jamming' and the 'pollution of the mental environment' by advertising. It is an entertaining read that also makes serious points about the way advertising tends to work by making people feel inadequate and dissatisfied with what they have, by creating new 'wants' rather than serving needs. Its images illuminate the emotional manipulation of much advertising, the symbiosis between eating disorders and the cosmetics and fashion industries, for example; the potentially desensitising effects of extended exposure to TV commercials. Calvin Klein, MacDonalds, Nike and Philip Morris are favoured targets of ad-busting critiques.

Throughout the 1990s, the Adbusters' parent organisation, the Media Foundation, has orchestrated an annual international 'No Shop Day'. It happens at the end of November – in America on the day after Thanksgiving, traditionally the biggest shopping day of the year, in Europe the next Saturday. Displays of performance art and street theatre sending up marketing hype and the shop-till-you-drop syndrome are sprung upon shoppers in malls in North America and Europe. The Manchester-based anti-consumerism group Enough organises the UK effort, although since last year the now-mainstream green campaigning organisation Friends of the Earth has supported and promoted the event among its 200,000 supporters here. Past events and street dramas have included 'puke-ins' outside fast food centres, people in period costumes seeking the ghostly remains of long-closed family-run shops put out of business by supermarkets, and 'doctors' dispensing advice from 'affluenza clinics'.

The impact on actual consumption is undoubtedly negligible, but TV, radio and newspaper coverage over the last couple of years has been considerable, given the relatively small number of agitators involved. Last year's No Shop Day antics were aired on the BBC Radio 4's *Today* programme and even given front page coverage in the *Wall Street Journal*.

What is interesting about the ploys used by Adbusters and No Shop Day activists is that they are beginning to plug the gaping holes in traditional environmental campaigning and strategies. The failure of environmentalists is not one of factual inaccuracy about the damage to human health and biodiversity wrought by modern mass production and consumption. Indeed, we owe them a huge debt. Without the research and investigation, lobbying and campaigning of environmental organisations, much of the destruction and exploitation would certainly remain unacknowledged and unchallenged by governments and businesses. But there has been a failure to shift consumer attitudes and to articulate the widespread dissatisfaction with the 'out of control' elements of consumerist culture that has been detected in recent attitudinal research.[2]

The failure is one of language and methods of communicating with a broad public audience. The language of modern environmentalism is a specialised one, used by and for experts and academics: sustainability, consumption, the 'triple bottom line', factor four, low-impact affluence, energy efficiency, renewables, recycleables. Of course all areas of specialist knowledge need jargon for their cogniscenti, but unless their essential elements can be translated into plain language, that is all they will remain: areas of specialist knowledge with no particular resonance for everyday debate and behaviour.

The consequence of this communication block leads to the second failure of modern environmentalism: its inability as yet to popularise its messages across income groups. The dynamics of the environmental movement and 'green' politics are still overwhelmingly middle class, middle-brow and middle England, and in that sense it tends to be socially exclusive rather than inclusive. Given the language in which its debates are couched, this is not surprising.

Although there is a growing awareness of these problems, the great challenge is to relate environmental goals to the psychological, social

2 See for example Macnaghten P et al, 1995, *Public Perceptions and Sustainability in Lancashire*, Lancashire County Council, Preston.

and cultural context in which they are expected to be achieved. This calls for much greater imagination on the part of campaigners for a more sustainable society about the kinds of social innovation that could break the grip of unsustainable consumerism on our consuming behaviour.

One example is the potential for new forms of mutual exchange. Where I live, in a small Wiltshire town, hundreds of us recently took part in Britain's first experiment in organised junk-swapping. Householders rummaged through their attics, garages and cupboards for unwanted clutter to offer with neighbours and friends one Sunday in July.

People deposited their offerings in front of their houses or brought them to the town's youth centre, which came to resemble a cashless car boot sale. Flower pots, books, sofas, baby car-seats, records, toys, pet cages, a homemade rowing machine and a plastic Christmas tree were among the free booty that changed hands. Old sofas and chairs were snapped up in the car park before their owners had even managed to haul them off their roof racks. Delighted children staggered home with armfuls of toys, books and folders for school. One boy was particularly chuffed at finding a shiny silver handbag to give to his mother.

The interesting point was that the main organisers, Wiltshire Agenda 21 and North Wiltshire District Council, avoided promoting the day primarily as an exercise in environmental improvement. They toyed with calling it 'Waste-Exchange' or 'Waste Swap' Day, but rightly concluded this might turn people off the idea. The focus of the 'Clear-Out Day', as it was eventually named, was on the social, practical and entertainment value of offering and getting something for nothing. If the day ultimately encouraged people to dwell on junk-swapping as a useful way to relieve pressure on landfill sites in particular and the environment in general, so much the better.

People who recycle waste regularly know that it tends to be a grim chore that usually requires travelling by car to a squalid corner of a car park to post your stuff into ugly containers that are either already overflowing. Turning the whole business into a potentially enjoyable and informative activity, something that is easy to do and which families, communities and neighbourhoods can do together would probably encourage more of us to do it. Just as the junk-swap event became a highly convivial gathering, as car-boot sales and the increasingly popular 'farmers' markets' for direct sale of farm produce in towns can also be, so recycling centres should be redesigned to encourage their 'congregational' potential.

If we are to swap profligate lifestyles for ones that are saner and more sustainable for ourselves, our surroundings and future generations, the benefits of such a transition need to be removed from the abstract realms of high policy debate and made tangible, direct and relevant to everyday life. They need to become seen as adding real value to our experiences, health, well-being, the way we work and relate to each other. Consumption, sustainability and community can and must go together: innovations such as 'adbusting' and the junk-swaping point the way to new forms of sustainable and convivial consumption beyond the increasingly unsatisfying 'must have' frenzy of traditional advertising-driven consumerism ⊙

Judy Jones is a journalist and writer on new forms of work, consumption and community development. She is the co-author, with Polly Ghazi, of Downshifting *(Coronet, 1997).*

© *Judy Jones 1998*

Senior services

Tessa Harding and **Mervyn Kohler** argue that entering the 'Third Age' and leading the good life are note incompatible if we tap the poetntial contribution of the elderly to society.

There is no such thing as 'the elderly'. It is an artificial category, a mere label for prejudice, not a reality. But we do have an ageing population, both in the UK and across the world, which usually conjures up a powerful image of dependency, poverty and greyness and sends some economists into anxiety over-drive. We look gloomily at the real increase in ill-health and disability, and worry about society's willingness and ability to fund pensions and pay for care.

Less frequently, we notice that older people play a considerable part in our national life, and that increased longevity has created the greatest pool of potential volunteers ever known in history. There is a huge wealth of energy, experience and knowledge waiting to be tapped. But neither the young nor the old in society really knows what to do with all this potential.

Today's older generation, being the first in this situation, has no role models to follow. As Eric Midwinter says, the 'Third Age' has yet to identify itself, to find its 'defining construct', and it lacks its 'seminal educators, designers, artists and narrators' who would help to create a sense of purpose and a 'cohesive lifestyle'[1]. (This is much less true in the United States, where reaching the age of 60 or 70 presents new opportunities to travel, to learn, to contribute to society in a different way.)

Meanwhile, the younger generations don't stop to think about the value of older people, or if they do, apply ageist stereotypes and assume that older people are out of touch, too slow – observers rather than actors. We set a basic pension level below Income Support and assume

1 Midwinter E in Bernard M and Phillips J, 1998, *The social policy of old age*, Centre for Policy on Ageing.

that older people have an acceptable quality of life even if they have barely enough food, warmth or a television.

But what makes for quality of life? One of the key factors is surely the confidence that we are known and appreciated by our fellow citizens, that we have something worthwhile to contribute to life and something useful and productive to do in the world. After retirement, that can be elusive.

When one takes a dispassionate look, there is actually quite a promising picture of growing old. Some older people simply don't stop what they are doing – writers and artists don't retire, and many people in public life simply continue to use their expertise and experience wearing a different hat. Others see retirement from paid work as the opportunity they have been waiting for to give their full attention to something new – a new area of interest, a new skill, a new career.

Yet others find new roles in their local community. We all know older people who say they are busier than they have ever been, that there aren't enough hours in the day and so on. They form the backbone of many membership institutions, from churches to political parties. Many are involved in the tiers of local government, where their local knowledge and their time is of priceless value. Above all, 'granny' is by far the largest childminding service in the country and older family and friends are what keep many disabled or sick people going. Older people are often the glue that holds the house of cards together and ensures that people 'get by'.

Margaret Simey[2] offers a vigorous new vision of the potential role of older people in society as essential contributors to the quality of life of the community as a whole. 'Politicians and administrators hopelessly underestimate the vital nature of the role of older people as a stabilising influence on both family life and on that of a society', she says. But to realise that role, age discrimination must go: 'only then will it be possible to explore the immense potential of the contribution that could and should be made to the promotion of our common welfare by the senior sector of our society.'

Achieving this potential, she argues, will require older people to take on new roles, responsibilities and obligations as active partners in the process of determining and implementing social policy. They will need help, and policy makers will need to act to remove the obstacles that stand in the way of such new roles at present – obstacles such as the 'habit of superiority'. She calls for 'a new emancipation movement that

2 Simey M in Bernard and Phillips, 1998 (note 1).

will set the elders of our community free to play their part in the challenging world of the technological revolution. Our mission as a society must be to bring older people out of the cold of dependency into the warmth of mainstream life in the community to our mutual benefit.' This is stirring stuff and a challenge to us all.

Removing barriers

What then are the barriers that need to be removed? First, it takes confidence, energy, opportunity and, yes, enough money to be able to carry on living life to the full without the structure of the world of work to support one. Too many things conspire at present to make such involvement difficult. Practical things like lack of money or lack of access to a car or reliable public transport get in the way. It is much harder to make a regular commitment to some community responsibility or personal project if one has to count the cost in pennies and essentials sacrificed in order to do so. And it is harder to be involved if the prospect of standing in the rain at a dark bus stop is daunting and energy-sapping before one has even begun. Making such ordinary down-to-earth things as money and transport more readily available and easier to access would remove the first barrier.

Second, the community structures that enable involvement themselves costs money – not necessarily a lot, but some. For at least a decade, the political establishment has been urging a growth of volunteering and community involvement. The prime minister has talked of volunteering as an aspect of citizenship, a good in its own right. But none of this rhetoric has gone into establishing budgets and a real revenue stream to stimulate such involvement. While the argument may have been won at an intellectual level, it has rarely borne tangible fruit.

That could change: we could fund the infrastructure that enables participation, at local level through the Better Government for Older People programme and other initiatives, and nationally through the Inter-Ministerial group on older people. In 1993, the European Year of Older People helped to create a glimpse of what older people could achieve by working together. It was a one-off event, so much of the momentum it generated has subsequently withered, but it remains a definitive example on how the potential of older people can be released. The 1999 UN Year of Older Persons offers a renewed opportunity.

Third, new technologies are going to be of huge significance. The opportunities presented by the Internet are just emerging, and those arising from digital broadcasting have not yet begun. We should be planning now to include older people in these developments so they can shape them to their own ends. There is every reason to believe that many older people will take to such new technologies like ducks to water, given the chance.

In this country, older people are experimenting with the possibilities of information technology, e-mail and video conferencing whenever a serious opportunity presents itself – a recent initiative in Wolverhampton that enabled the local Pensioners' Forum to link up with older people in other European countries is a case in point. In the US, meanwhile, where access to personal computers is much more widespread and well-established, seniors are the fastest growing group of Internet users. And why not? The Internet brings a wealth of interest, information and discovery into your own front room.

But of course new technology has benefits to offer beyond information. The development of 'smart homes', assistive devices and electronic safety features can all help older people whose mobility, strength or energy is restricted to continue to live independently and more comfortably, given the resources to make these innovations available.

Above all, it is our attitudes and expectations that need to change. A culture that sees older people only as recipients, and denies and devalues their roles and their individuality, will never unlock their potential. That culture runs deep and affects the full range of services, from adult education to stigmatising social care.

The recent initiative on 'lifelong learning' and the green paper 'The Learning Age', for example, focus exclusively on people of working age, ignoring the potential offered by a good fifth of the population each of whom has up to 30 years of active life experience. Most day centres and care packages offered to older people concentrate exclusively on the safety and maintenance of their recipients, rather than on their continued involvement in the things that interest and motivate them. The health service, which has concentrated ever more narrowly on cure rather than on promoting good health, rehabilitation following illness and maximising the potential of those with long-term conditions, is failing to contribute adequately to the quality of life of older people. The full range of our community services needs to spend time and effort talking to older users and find out just how much could be done, often at minimal cost, to promote their involvement and develop their potential.

There has been a revolution over the past 20 years in our attitudes towards people with physical disabilities or learning difficulties. It is no longer acceptable to consign them to institutions or limit their aspirations. Disabled people have fought for and achieved the right to manage their own assistance through direct payments, so that they can organise their lives themselves according to their own aspirations – and it has been a real liberation for many. The same kind of revolution is needed with regard to services for older people, so that such services support and encourage autonomy, individuality and inclusion – rather than assuming that a standard package, in which the user has little choice or control, will do.

Rather than assuming that what an older population will need is 'more of the same', let us instead start from the proposition that we will support the ideas and initiatives that older people themselves promote, and not attempt to unroll a programme designed elsewhere and reflecting other people's values. It's time we handed responsibility, opportunity and respect back to the older generation and let them get on with it ⊙

Tessa Harding is Head of the Policy Unit at Help the Aged.

Mervyn Kohler is Head of Public Affairs at Help the Aged.

Friendly society

Professor Ray Pahl argues that market societies would be happier if we took the cultivation of friendship more seriously.

Fuelled by ambition and measured by money, often later translated into status and power, success has been more worshipped than analysed for more than two hundred years. To be sure, the early sociologists recognised the problem. Max Weber remarked how irrational it was from the viewpoint of personal happiness for a man to exist for the sake of his business, instead of the reverse. Likewise Emil Durkheim remarked in his classic study on suicide that 'over-weening ambition always exceeds the results of obtained... this race for an unattainable goal can give no other pleasure but that of the race itself, if it is one. Once it is interrupted the participants are left empty handed'.[1] Writing in 1896, Durkheim feared the consequences of the 'almost infinite extension of the market' leading to an endless thirst for change and novelty.

> 'The wise man, knowing how to enjoy achieved results without having constantly to replace them with others, finds in them an attachment to life in the hour of difficulty. But the man who has always pinned all his hopes on the future and lived with his eyes fixed upon it, has nothing in the past as a comfort against the present's afflictions, for the past was nothing to him but a series of hastily experienced stages. What blinded him to himself was his expectation always to find further on the happiness he had so far missed. Now he is stopped in his tracks; from now on nothing remains behind or ahead of him to fix his gaze upon. Weariness alone, moreover, is enough to bring disillusionment, for he cannot in the end escape the futility of an endless pursuit'.[2]

1 Durkheim E, 1952 [1896], *Suicide*, Routledge, London.
2 See note 1.

Such concerns are matched by a fear of success which has been explored as much by the ancient Greek philosophers as the Freudians and the post-Freudians. The fear of success can be as psychologically damaging as an obsessive compulsion towards it.

Stimulated by such ideas, I interviewed some of the most overtly successful men and women in British society to explore the ambiguities, anxieties, neuroses and frustrations of success. Among these people I found a fortunate few who are not overburdened by self-doubts, who are pre-eminent in their fields and who are enjoying their lives. These were people who did not take *themselves* too seriously but who undertook what they had to do seriously. They learned to play so they may be serious.

Some would say that the secret of happiness is to get enjoyment out of what you have to do. That might imply that work has to be absorbing, to be fun, perhaps, even, to be close to play. Sociologists have long noted the distinctions between instrumental and affective attitudes to work. Happiness does not necessarily come more from seeing work as a means to an end (getting money to enjoy conviviality elsewhere, for example) than as an end in itself (the creative artist or craftsman).

Many readers of this issue of *Collection* might be inclined to leave the question of happiness to religious leaders or psychoanalysts. Why bother with this issue now when British society as a whole is seemingly more rich and prosperous compared with the grey post-war years? The answer is that there is much evidence to support the claim that 'Since the mid 1960s there has been an unprecedented increase in clinical depression in advanced and rapidly advancing economies'.[3] It is gradually becoming more widely accepted and discussed among sociologists that people's prime experience of the market economy as producers or employees is not, on balance, a happy one, secondly that patterns of consumption exacerbate a debilitating social malady and, thirdly, that one of the most important causes of depression is the lack of friends or confidants – a decline in social support. Analysts of various epidemiological studies are coming to common agreement that people in richer countries are getting more depressed. Lane quotes one authoritative study claiming that 'People born after 1945 were ten times more likely to suffer from depression than people born 50 years earlier'.[4] He claims that studies of increasing mood disorders in children are even more disturbing as it appears that childhood depression is a strong indicator of later depression in adulthood.

3 Lane D, 1991, *The Market Experience*, Cambridge; Lane D, 1994, 'The road not taken', *The Critical Review Fall*, 521-554.
4 See note 3.

There is little evidence to suggest that the rich are any happier than the less rich: once one moves beyond the poverty level, as Adam Smith remarked, 'In ease of body and mind, all the ranks of life are nearly upon a level'. That being so, we should not necessarily expect the materially successful to be that much happier nor able to tell as much about the ingredients of happiness.

A newly emerging question is whether there is something distinctive about what is happening to friendship in contemporary society which is directly affecting our happiness and quality of life. It is my contention that there are certain aspects of contemporary society that are inimical to true friendships as opposed to the shallower instrumental kinds of relationships so avidly collected by the networker or socialite. Yet, paradoxically, there are other tendencies that are encouraging and developing these close, supportive social links that are leaving people to grow in happiness and emotional depth in a way that is not so easy in a society which is more formally structured in terms of traditional gender, kin and workplace roles.

Paradoxically again, it seems that higher levels of material development which lead to higher income per head have potentially greater impact on the happiness of the poor than that of the rich. At higher levels of income, friends and friendship are a better and well-established ingredient of greater happiness and of preventing, or perhaps even curing, depression. Thus, the rich who in their fevered race for success may have less time for their friends may thus add to their own depression but, with appropriate redistributive policies, they may at least help to alleviate some of the burdens of the poor, although this might not cheer them up. But if the materially successful recognise the unintended consequences of their strivings, would they be so keen to strive? Is it not in the interests of the poor to drive the richer into stress and depression in the competitive market economy and then collectively to support substantial redistributive taxation?

If indeed it is the case that, as Lane argues, it is the loss or absence of companionship, friends and satisfying, enduring family relationships that accounts for a substantial part of the rise in depression, why have the more affluent been so misguided? Why have so many chosen the consumption of things over the cultivation of friendship? Do people, as Marx suggested, pursue more wealth to compensate for failed friendships or disappointment in love, only to find that more money fails to satisfy? These are some of the issues that Daniel Bell explored in *The Cultural Contradictions of Capitalism*.[5]

In order to assess the grand theories of social malaise in contemporary society it is not enough to measure the *quantity* of peoples' relationships in micro-social worlds. The quality of such relationships has to be explored and understood as well. This is the focus of my current research and it is not an easy task.

Survey research suggests that since 1960 there has been a steady downward trend in the percentage of respondents who said they trust 'most people'. This, it is suggested, undermines social support. Lane and others argue that it is the market in general and the 'rage to consume' in particular, that have crowded out or undermined friendship.

This is a very gloomy perspective and not one that can be easily dispelled. The consumer society is unlikely to go away. However, there are signs that people are more inclined to give priority to friends and friend-like relations. They recognise the importance of friends for help in a crisis, such as divorce or when afflicted with AIDs or similar serious illnesses. Children leave home, parents die, partners split-up but some friends can provide continuity and identity support through the turmoils of life. As people come to recognise the value of friends for finding jobs, reducing stress, warding off depression and much else besides, they might come to value an alternative model of success: as St Thomas Aquinas put it, 'Pleasure lies in being, not becoming'. As I show in my book, some people can balance different forms of success to achieve both wealth and happiness – these are exceptional people.[6] For many there is more likely a self destructive obsessional neurosis driving them on.

One way to create a happier – and indeed more healthier – society would be to increase the space in which people could find more friendship and social support. People who feel obliged to work very long hours may be disabling themselves. Some recent psychological research indicates having a greater sense of control in life can be as positive for well-being and reducing depression as social support is. Indeed, the one can take the place of the other.

Market societies could, therefore, be much happier and levels of clinical depression would be reduced if people had more personal control over their lives and their opportunities for developing friendships were increased. Much of this relates to the way we organise our work and employment. If people are not trusted, if they are endlessly checked,

5 Bell D, 1976, *The Cultural Contradictions of Capitalism*, Heinemann, London.
6 Pahl R, 1995, *After Success*, Polity Press, Cambridge.

observed, measured, assessed, reported on and endlessly obliged to conform to externally imposed rules, regulations and controls, one might find that in the end it got them down. They become miserable, depressed and a further charge on the NHS.

Maybe when the Social Exclusion Unit has run its course in Downing Street, the prime minister might consider establishing a Happiness Unit. Who knows, this might do more for the well-being of the British population than could ever be optimistically proposed in a political manifesto ⊙

Professor Ray Pahl is at the Centre on Micro-Social Change, University of Essex. His books include After Success *(Polity Press, 1995).*

Communities of good practice

Membership of community associations can deliver benefits for individuals and society. **Bronislaw Szerszynski** explores the good life as promoted by 'lifestyle communities'.

Understanding the good life through lifestyles

One of the starting points of this collection is the growing sense that public life in modern societies is too dominated by a 'thin' picture of the good life, measured in terms of material consumption and security, with negative consequences for both environmental sustainability and human fulfilment. Such claims are consistent with the findings of research carried out since 1991 at Lancaster University's Centre for the Study of Environmental Change (CSEC). Using qualitative social research methods such as focus groups, we have been exploring the complex cultural dimensions – all too often overlooked – of people's concerns and experience in relation to environmental and risk issues such as nuclear power and genetic engineering, countryside forestry and leisure, sustainable development and global environmental responsibility.

Most of this research has been designed to capture the mood of 'the public' – or sections of the public – in relation to such issues. Accordingly, people have been picked at random according to demographic criteria – age, gender, residence, occupation and so on – and brought together in ways that have encouraged them to speak as representatives of these wider demographic groups. In such research, people overwhelmingly report a sense of powerlessness and isolation, a mistrust of institutions in both the public and private sectors, and a profound anxiety about the future. In doing so, they are describing how, despite all their best attempts, their lives fail to measure up to the dominant idea of the good life referred to above.

However, some of the research conducted at CSEC has taken a rather different approach, bringing together in its discussion groups people who share not demographic characteristics, but lifestyle practices. Some of these have been what might be called radical subcultures – members of communes and of radical campaigning groups – but others have been groups whose members are in other ways unexceptional – members of leisure-based subcultures such as cyclists, or of health self-help groups, for example. What has been striking about the findings generated by these pieces of research has been the way that a much richer and more complex alternative picture emerges of what it might be to live a good and flourishing life in contemporary society.

How can this contrast be explained? One explanation is simply that some people – those who belong to clear lifestyle communities or 'communities of practice' – have a richer sense of the good life than others. Another explanation is that if you bring *anyone* together with other people who share the same enthusiasms and passions as them, then those things will be brought to the fore, and you will find out what they 'really' think and care about. Either way, this is consistent with the historical thesis that a solid idea of the good life has not disappeared from contemporary society, but has fragmented into the burgeoning number of lifestyle communities that make up the complex plural cultures of advanced capitalist societies. In the post-war period, there may have been a broad public consensus about the good life, in terms of a model of citizenly behaviour and a rich and cultured life. But such a consensus, which sustained and was sustained by a sense of belonging to a wider civic community of shared values, has broken down. People's notions of human fulfilment are increasingly shaped and sustained not by the communities into which they are thrown by accident of birth, but by the communities to which they choose to belong. Given this, it would perhaps not be surprising to find that it is when you bring people together in such chosen social groupings, rather than in the more 'accidental' ones thrown up by demographic criteria, that a richer picture of the 'good life' emerges.

What are lifestyle communities?

What sort of things would count as 'lifestyle communities' or 'communities of practice' in the way I'm using the terms here? One problem with defining such terms is that during the past few decades cultural changes have rendered inadequate many of the received dis-

tinctions between different kinds of social activity and between different kinds of social groupings. Distinctions that were once relatively
easy to make – such as between style subcultures and political movements, leisure activities and ethical movements, health and spiritual-
ity, acts of consumption and of citizenship – are coming to seem
increasingly problematic. Similarly, where once the boundaries of communities were reasonably easy to draw, increased geographical, social
and cultural mobility, rapid developments in both personal and mass
communications media and complex patterns of cultural globalisation
have meant that the social networks with which people most identify
are often stretched and dispersed across space and time.

On the other hand, it is clearly important not to lose sight of the
important contrasts between different kinds of chosen social memberships. Indeed, increased mobility and mass communication has if
anything increased rather than decreased the range of different kinds
of community, and ways in which people can actually be said to
'belong' to them. Some – like tennis clubs, reading groups, credit unions
or animal rights groups – are generally very local in flavour, caught
up with the daily and weekly life of some, generally urban, place.
Others, by contrast, are far more dispersed, such as e-mail discussion
lists and, increasingly, friendship networks. Similarly, while all of the
above might generally consist of people who are known to each other,
a wholly different set of dispersed communities to which we might
belong (pressure group memberships, ethical shoppers, hobbyists)
might be made up largely of people who are actually strangers to us.
Rather than experiencing such communities through interactions with
particular others, whether proximate or distant, they exist for us more
as 'imagined communities', other members of which we rarely get to
know or even communicate with.

Similarly, lifestyle communities can also be discriminated in terms
of the kind of 'in-order-to' which initially brings people into the group.
Some chosen memberships are at root simply that – chosen, from a
range of possibilities, on the basis of what we want to do. At the core
of such leisure or hobby subcultures is the idea of the pursuit of pleasure, not that of profit or the ethical life. Other communities of practice, however, are joined more out of need than out of choice – the self-
help group, the baby-sitting circle, the credit union or the dispersed
community of users of alternative medicine, for example. Yet other
shared practices, such as direct action, charitable work or ethical

lifestyles, are taken up primarily for ethical or political reasons – out of a sense not that 'I want', or that 'I need', but that 'I ought'.

However, over time the reasons that people belong to such chosen social groupings can change in subtle ways. For example, someone might join a reading group or a badminton club for social reasons, but become increasingly fascinated and absorbed by the complex internal details of the activity itself. Someone else might be propelled by an individual 'conversion experience' to join an animal rights group, but find themselves drawn into an intense network of friendships, perhaps adopting a new lifestyle, with distinctive patterns of dress and musical taste. Someone might join a self-help group as a means to finding ways to cope with a chronic illness, but become more interested in the intrinsic pleasures of organising a civic group, or in the sheer experience of political agency, of being able to effect changes in wider society. Such changes, I suggest, can be understood in terms of how people's picture of the good and fulfilling life can be shaped by the experience of belonging to 'communities of practise' such as these.

The benefits of lifestyle communities

In what way can people's membership of chosen communities such as lifestyle coalitions, associations and movements actually *deliver* a sense of living a good and rewarding life? How might membership of such communities produce people who seek a richer and more sustainable set of goods, goods which accumulate not as a store of physical possessions, but as a deepening life narrative and set of human capacities? There are perhaps two different kinds of answer to this. The first is to say that *membership of a community of practice can serve as a means by which people can acquire particular quality-of-life goods which are difficult if not impossible to obtain as an individual.*

Perhaps the most obvious of these 'associational goods' is sociality itself, the sheer pleasure of interacting with other human beings. But even this seemingly simple notion is refracted into countless hues by the particular shared activities and meanings sustained by different communities of practice. Encountering another person as a co-participant in a particular shared practice – a jazz improvisation, say, a football match or a political protest – represents quite a different way of encountering each other as human beings. On one level, such interactions alone seem to afford only a very partial way of knowing what another human being is like. But at times we want to say that they give us glimpses of what people are 'really' like, glimpses of their character that would be almost impossible to have outside the context of that shared practice – or to describe to someone who does not have any experience of that practice. Similarly, a chance meeting with a fellow member of a community of practice – a fellow cyclist, vegan or stamp collector, for example – can give an intense experience of comradeship, fuelled partly by the sheer scarcity value of finding someone who has made the same lifestyle choices in a highly pluralistic society.

But belonging to a community of practice can also deliver to its members other, perhaps less obvious, classes of associational good. One consists of the skills and knowledge that can be acquired through membership. Sometimes such capacities necessarily remain more or less internal to the practice – an intense knowledgeability about *Star Trek*, for example, is of little use outside the bounds of the 'Trekkie' community. But other skills and knowledges are eminently transferable from their original associational crucible to the wider civic realm – members of self-help groups can gain extraordinary organisational and literacy skills, for example, and martial arts practitioners acquire new levels of personal discipline and self-control, all of which are personal capacities with wider civic value.

Yet another group of associational goods is connected with issues of identity, agency and virtue. The local community that organises itself to oppose the construction of a new land fill site may fail in its overt objective, but win the perhaps greater prize of increased self-awareness and purposefulness as a community. Volunteers for local charities can gain pleasure themselves from doing good in the community – a form of motivation that is often cynically decried, rather than valued as an added benefit of voluntary work. Finally, another class of associational good consists of what are sometimes called 'internal goods' – goods that are defined in terms of the internal rules of a practice, rather than by reference to external benefits, and are closely linked to the criteria by which excellence at that activity is measured.

This notion links closely to the research into human happiness conducted by the psychologist Csikszentmihalyi. The 'flow' experience, identified as the peak of human happiness by Csikszentmihalyi, is one that is characteristically achieved during the absorbed, proficient performance of shared human activities. The basketball players, climbers and musicians that experience such 'flow' do so as individuals – but do so overwhelmingly in the context of shared sets of practices, rules and meanings which are sustained over time by a wider community of practitioners.

It is clear, then, that membership of communities of practice can deliver a broad range of quality-of-life goods in a way that can make them highly pertinent to any transition to a more sustainable society. These 'softer' goods are capable of providing happiness and fulfilment in ways whose side effects are more in the form of increases in human and social capital than decreases in natural capital. But associations and lifestyle communities also play a second, subtler role in the fostering of alternative versions of the good life. They can serve not just as instruments for the delivery of quality-of-life goods to individuals, but as *communities that provide and sustain a view of life in which such 'softer' goods appear desirable in the first place.*

This is an important distinction. I argued above that, through engaging in shared practices with others, individuals can obtain associational goods which might form the components of a more sustainable vision of the good life than that which dominates wider consumer culture. However, why should they value such softer goods as sociality, skill and virtue over the harder goods offered by consumerism? Why should they see the project of creating a deepening life-narrative, a life understood as a quest for the good life, as of any value at all?

In order to value associational goods as components of the good life, it would seem, people would already have to at least glimpse the larger framework within which such valuations would make sense. This is where the second role of lifestyle communities comes in – they serve as 'minority sects', keeping alive alternative visions of the good life, or what the philosopher Charles Taylor calls 'frameworks of strong evaluation', by which we judge some choices to be more worthwhile than others. And, for those who come to embrace such visions, lifestyle communities offer new social networks that can support the lifestyle changes that can follow from a change in priorities. As Michael Jacobs of the Fabian Society points out, it is unreasonable to expect individuals to change to more ecologically friendly lifestyles without the existence of new social networks to replace the old ones from which they will likely be severing themselves by such changes.

Conclusion

I have suggested that contemporary lifestyle pluralism should not be regarded *pessimistically*, as symptom and cause of our loss of all but the thinnest possible shared picture of the good life and human fulfilment, but *optimistically*, as a cultural condition that helps to ensure that alternative pictures of the good life continue to be available. Rather than seeing cultural fragmentation as a postmodern abandonment of civility, we might thus regard it more hopefully, as making possible a different way of being 'civil'. This fragile, emergent, pluralised mode of citizenship is one that is characterised by a cosmopolitan *awareness* of difference, rather than a monolithic belief in one form of life as the pinnacle of social evolution. However, whether the social spaces in which this new civility might be nurtured will continue to flourish, or whether they will be crushed by global consumerism or by social policies informed by narrow and outmoded understandings of people's loyalties and social identities, remains to be seen ⊙

Bronislaw Szerszynski, sociologist and philosopher, is Lecturer at the Centre for the Study of Environmental Change, Lancaster University. He is co-editor of Risk, Environment and Modernity *(Sage, 1996).*

Virtuous realities

Marianne Talbot argues that we need a rigorous programme of education to equip young people to lead ethical good lives and think coherently about values.

'It is the one who screws the customer who gets the Porsche,' I was told when I gave a talk on values to a meeting of the RSA's Forum for Ethics in the Workplace. The person who said it was caricaturing the view that 'the good life' is constituted by Porsche ownership, and the means to the good life involves doing whatever is necessary. It is not the main aim of this essay to argue against this view but rather to identify a few of the key ingredients of an education that would fit people for the good life as I understand it: a life lived in accordance with the Kantian absolute 'each of us should treat himself and others never merely as a means, but always at the same time as an end.'[1] I shall also draw out the policy implications of my claims and a major difficulty currently facing anyone trying to educate the young for the good life.

To treat someone – including oneself – as an end rather than as a means to an end is to treat them as a rational, autonomous, happiness-loving human being, as someone who acts for reasons (even if these are not apparent), who has their own goals (even if they seem to be daft), who has responsibility, ultimately, for their own happiness and, at least potentially, the rights and duties of one human being among others.

This account of the good life is wholly consistent with Aristotle's claim that the good life, given luck,[2] is a life lived in accordance with the virtues.[3] It takes courage to allow others to make their own choices, integrity to avoid self-deception, prudence and temperance to make provision for one's future well-being, and a just nature to see that rights bring with them duties to recognise the same rights for others. Those who engage in the practice mentioned in the first paragraph are

1 Kant I, 1948, *Groundwork of the Metaphysic of Morals*, translated by HJ Paton as *The Moral Law*, Routledge, London.

2 Aristotle believed that bad luck – for example, the loss of one's family in an accident – would make the good life impossible, even if all other conditions were satisfied.

3 Aristotle, *The Nicomachean Ethics*, especially book one.

damaging their chances of living the good life because they are failing to recognise that the good life depends on secure relationships with others and on the sort of integrity that can be achieved only by one who has nothing to hide. Those who aim for the Porsche, oblivious to goods of this sort, have a conception of the good so impoverished as to be unworthy of the name. So, what sort of education will fit young people to achieve the good life?

Importantly, I do not mean by 'education' only what goes on in schools and colleges. Education goes on whenever a person's curiosity is aroused, their desire for an explanation stimulated and their senses and intelligence engaged in a systematic and sustained search for understanding. No one is truly being educated unless they are an active participant in the process.

This leads me to one of the key ingredients of an education for the good life – it must be *inspirational* as well as *instrumental*. 'If you don't do it you won't get a job' is a counsel of despair, an admission that the attempt to educate has failed. Teachers who *live* the fact they value their subject, parents whose enjoyment of life is evident, managers whose commitment is palpable, are all educating their charges in the truest sense of the word.

But enthusiasm, of course, can be misdirected. And here is the second key ingredient of an education for the good life – it must encourage a critical stance, one that mitigates against the uncritical acceptance of the Porsche version of the good life. Not everything that *is* valued is, in fact, *valuable*. Discovering what *is* good, rather than what simply *appears* to be good, depends on a preparedness to question one's own beliefs and those of others in the search for truth, and on the ability to engage, with tenacity, in effective argument. The first depends on humility, on an openness to discovering that one is wrong, the second on courage and sensitivity: it is not always easy to say that one believes someone is wrong without upsetting them. Unless we are willing and able to do this, however, we risk dissolving in a sea of frothy relativism. I shall argue below that this relativism is the most serious obstacle facing anyone who wants education to fit young people for the good life.

Humility, tenacity, integrity, courage – it starts to sound old-fashioned. But consider another key ingredient of an education for the good life: the promotion of self-confidence and the integrity on which true self-confidence[4] depends.

4 The qualifier 'true' is intended to distinguish self-confidence from the arrogance of bullies, often the result of a lack of self-esteem. One who is truly confident of their own worth has no need to bully others.

Self-confidence, like sleep, is not something for which we can strive in its own right, we achieve it only by achieving something else. In the case of sleep, peace of mind is required; in the case of self-confidence we need a robust set of values and the ability to live up to those values. Our values constitute our beliefs about the nature of the good life. They also constrain our pursuit of our goals; to the extent that we value truth, for example, we will believe that it is wrong to lie even to achieve something else we want.

So our values make demands on us, they are ideals, and living up to them is not easy. To live up to one's values generates self-liking and a confidence in one's own worth. Failing to live up to them results in shame and lack of self-respect. Our values, and our ability to live up to them, are also linked to *others'* views of us, to our reputation. Insofar as we fail to 'walk our talk' others will learn not to trust us and this is inimical to good relationships.

This brings us to the final key ingredient in an education for the good life: the need to encourage self-discipline. Nearly all the good things of life, excepting those whose enjoyment we share with animals, are attained only through the exercise of self-discipline. The virtues, moral and intellectual, must also be practised daily if we are to acquire a secure hold on them.

The education needed to fit young people to achieve the good life, then, is inspirational and not just instrumental, it encourages a critical stance, fosters self-confidence by instilling a robust set of values and enhances the likelihood of a person's living up to these values by encouraging self-discipline in the habit of the virtues, moral and intellectual.

But are we, as a society, providing our young people with such an education? To answer this it is best to look first at a major problem facing our society.

This problem is that of an ill-thought through relativism, cognitive and moral. This relativism consists, roughly speaking, in the view that all truth is relative to an individual, that there is no such thing as truth independent of us, but only truth-for-me, truth-for-you, or at best truth-for-us. This relativism is the result of the false belief that arguing with someone, or implying in any way that they are wrong, means failing to respect them.

To see that this belief is false we need only consider that a willingness to argue with someone, to say that they are wrong and to 'fight it out' (in the nicest possible way) is a sign of good friendship. To claim to believe that someone is right when we disagree with them is patronising in the extreme, or it is self-denying in that we treat our own views as unimportant.

Argument – friendly and engaged argument – is the means by which rational animals collaborate in the search for truth. But the possibility of argument depends on a willingness to say to another that one believes they are wrong, and to be told, by others, that they believe us to be wrong. Yet the idea that telling someone they are wrong is likely to lead to a crisis of self-confidence (or that it is the sign of an imposition of spurious authority) is endemic in education. This can only lead – indeed it *has* led – to a generation who put an ill thought-out 'respect for others' above the collaborative search for truth.

One educational manifestation of the idea that to tell someone they are wrong will lead to a crisis in confidence can be seen in some teachers' refusal to mark errors in pupils' work, or their insistence on marking only some errors. I once listened to a class of thirteen year olds taking turns to read aloud and was horrified as pupil after pupil made errors that went unmentioned by the teacher. I was told that this was because I was there and that it would do pupils' confidence no good to be told they were wrong in front of a visitor.[5]

Many teachers, of course, understand the importance of marking errors and they mark them despite the prevailing view. Such teachers, however, have had to face a crisis of confidence – *am* I doing the right thing? *Might* I be damaging my pupils? Such concerns generate a tentativity, a lack of confidence, that is inimical to good teaching.

The current concern about academic standards will have an effect on the disastrous idea as it manifests itself in subjects such as English and mathematics. But there is an area in which it is less visible, an area which, if it is allowed to go unchecked, could be even more damaging to our society. This is the area of morality.

I have students who will not say that Hitler was wrong. They say that they don't like what he did or that they wouldn't do it themselves, but they won't say that he was wrong. When asked why, they say things like 'everyone is entitled to their own moral views' or 'who am I to question someone else's morality?'. This is the disastrous idea writ large, amounting to the claim that in morality 'anything goes'.

There is a different but equally benign thought behind the disastrous idea in the area of morality. This is the idea that we should recognise and celebrate diversity. The need to do this is a corrective to the time

5 The sort of errors being made – some of which made a nonsense of the sentences in which they appeared – suggests this could not be the whole story.

when to be anything other than a middle-aged white male was to go uncounted. But we go too far if, in our rush to recognise and celebrate diversity, we forget the many and equally important similarities between us, not least our shared core values.

We also go too far if we think that *all* diversity is to be celebrated. Some differences between us ought to be deplored and discouraged *because* of the values we share and because all human beings are intrinsically valuable. Even the Hitlers and Fred Wests, after all, are accorded a fair trial and subjected to no 'cruel and unusual punishment'. Despite their actions they were human beings and to fail to treat them as such would be to demean ourselves, to act as less than human. But this does not mean that they were right to think and do what they thought and did.

It is quite wrong to say that there are no common values.[6] However pluralist our society, our common humanity and our common need for a peaceful society ensure that there are many values we share. And if there are common values, then our children have the same rights and duties to understand and live up to these values as they have to understand and follow the rules of grammar. We fail in our duty to the young if we allow them to think that anything goes in the area of values, just as much as we fail in our duty if we allow them to think that anything goes in grammar.

Finally, there are policy recommendations to be drawn. First, the government should explicitly recognise the existence and importance of common values by stimulating a society-wide debate about these values, the common good life. This should not be a 'back to basics' campaign or indeed any campaign that tries to *impose* a certain set of values, because no such thing is needed. There *are* common values and that there are becomes obvious the minute people start to discuss the question. It is the very discussion of such issues that leads to people becoming aware of these values and to a true understanding of their importance to us.

The approach of the millennium provides the ideal time to start such a debate. It is a natural time for us to reflect on where we are, where we are going and whether we are going in the right direction. The Millennium Dome could be put to excellent use here: what better celebration of the human spirit than a vigorous debate about one of the features that distinguishes us from animals – the ability to value things for their own sake and to construct a pluralist community

6 The National Forum for Values in Education and the Community, set up by the School Curriculum and Assessment Authority in 1996, provided empirical evidence for this. This forum, consisting of 150 adults drawn from across society, drafted a list of values they believed would be agreed on by everyone. MORI sent this draft to 3,200 schools, 700 national organisations and did an omnibus poll of 1,500 adults. Between 87 and 95 per cent of respondents agreed to the values outlined, as did the leaders of all main faiths groups in the country.

around such values?

The government should not be put off stimulating such a debate by either of two (inconsistent) claims made by opponents of such initiatives. The first claim – that this is a pluralist society in which there are no common values – is the result of too concentrated a focus on conflict and the bad. Most people in our society are, generally speaking, trustworthy, kind, caring and willing to search for agreement. Acts of viciousness, or even dishonesty, are much more unusual. This is why, in fact, we are a 'good news is no news' society, a society that struggles to see the good because we constantly focus on the bad. The second – that common values are so obvious and so anodyne that there is no point in identifying them – is seen to be false by the way that the first view has managed to undermine our belief in the shared values on which society depends. Shared values are the glue that hold our society together: they *are* obvious, but perhaps they are *so* obvious that we have forgotten they exist.

Second, the government should act decisively to counter the lazy thinking that is behind the spread of the knee-jerk relativism outlined above. It is quite extraordinary that, despite the expertise in logic – critical thinking – that exists in our universities, this subject makes next to no appearance in our schools and is not taught as an essential tool to teachers. Logic should be taught to every teacher during initial teacher training and it should be made available to trained teachers through programmes of continuing professional development. The ability to recognise and evaluate arguments, to identify fallacies (bad arguments that masquerade as good ones) and an awareness of the need to offer good reasons for one's claims are a *sine qua non* in an age where there is so much information around, one of the most important things people can learn is how to evaluate and use this information.

Importantly, the teaching of logic should not be confined to the 'hard' subjects. In personal and social education and in citizenship education, moral reasoning should be taught. It should be taught in such a way that it is clearly continuous with the sort of critical thinking that goes on in other disciplines – that is, with concern for truth, tenacity and rigour. The beauty of logic and skills in reasoned argument is that they are 'topic-neutral', working in the same way for every subject. This makes them, of course, the ultimate transferable skills and ones our children deserve to acquire.

That we have allowed ourselves to accept a sterile position of relativism in so many areas of political and social life is a sad indictment of education. Our neglect of the ability to reason – another feature that distinguishes us from animals – is quite extraordinary. The explanation of this is presumably the dearth of people who are capable of teaching it. If we were to bite the bullet and train more such people we would be repaid many times over by the fact that we would end up with a population far less likely to engage in the sort of woolly thinking, especially about morality and the good, that enables them to form the impoverished conception of the good with which I started this essay: a conception that can only lead to the sort of deathbed regrets that signify a wasted life ⊙

Marianne Talbot is a Lecturer in Philosophy at Oxford University, a Consultant to the Qualifications and Curriculum Authority and an adviser to the National Forum for Values in Education and the Community.

Bookmarks

The morality of happiness

Julia Annas

In this meticulous and wide-ranging study of the moral thought of classical and Hellenistic Greece, Annas demonstrates the coherence and contemporary relevance of ancient ideas of human fulfilment. Far from being merely egoistic or aesthetic and lacking truly moral content, she shows that ancient ideas of human flourishing offer ways of understanding intimate connections between the virtues and the fulfilled life. Where modern moral thought is expected to deliver specific and defensible general answers to dilemmas where principles conflict, ancient ethics was more concerned with the character of the life in which decent and fulfilled people could find their own practical resolutions to moral conflicts, rather than to prescribe rules by which they should resolve them. Contrary to the fashionable view that ancient thought is irrevocably strange, no longer relevant to contemporary debates about the good life and perhaps not even concerned with morality in the modern sense at all, Annas's study shows that we can hardly expect to understand our own conceptions of fulfilment or the moral life without appreciating their roots. Long and not an easy read, but worth persevering with.

(Oxford University Press, 1993)

Moral wisdom and good lives

John Kekes

Most moral philosophers, when asked about the good life, will either invoke rules to live by – categorical imperatives, maximising utility and so on – or else describe sets of institutions that make good lives possible – institutions of distributive justice or those which make for some idea of social decency. Kekes, however, develops his earlier account of how the objective basis of moral ideas can be reconciled with the recognition of a reasonable and limited pluralism, to base his idea of the good life on the practice of moral wisdom, self-knowledge, moral imagination and commitment. The book offers one of the most sustained efforts to integrate virtue ethics with a genuinely pluralist account of human flourishing. Readable to non-philosophers, thoughtful and provocative.

(Cornell University Press, Ithaca, New York, 1995)

Well-being: its meaning, measurement and moral importance

James Griffin

A comprehensive study of the philosophical issues around well-being, which explores the scope and limits of the utilitarianism that falls so naturally into Anglo-Saxon debates about public policy and the good life. Griffin examines in some detail the possibility of reconciling morality with practical reason through arguments about well-being. Not always well-organised and sometimes prolix, but valuable.

(Oxford University Press, Oxford, 1986)

The quality of life

Amartya Sen, Martha Nussbaum, eds

Shelf-breaking collection of major essays by international big stars with a strong North American bias. The first section explores the implications of Sen's argument that the quality of life is to be measured not in terms of subjective well-being or satisfaction, but in terms of the capabilities achieved but individuals, and what this might mean for arguments about inequality. Philosophical issues are discussed, before turning to debates about gender and the question of whether women seek quality of life in different ways from men. The book closes with a discussion of policy issues concerning measurement of the standard of living and health status. Essential reading for those interested in theoretical issues, but not easy going; the sum of its parts.

(Oxford University Press, Oxford, 1993)

How are we to live? Ethics in an age of self-interest

Peter Singer

For too long, Singer argues, our conception of the good life has been bound up with narrow self-interest and measured against material wealth and consumption, and it is generally thought that an ethical life equals self-sacrifice. This illuminating and original examination of how we should live succeeds in undercutting the supposed conflict between self-interest and ethics to show that, far from resulting in denial and discontent, an ethical life is a life with meaning. Via a wide-ranging study encompassing religious, philosophical, political and Darwinian explanations of how human nature and society operate, Singer convincingly demonstrates that the modern Western trend of seeking fulfilment by looking inwards, exemplified in the ever-growing therapy industry, is essentially flawed. The ultimate message of this genuinely life-changing book is that only by looking outwards, and viewing fulfilment as contingent upon contributing to the greater good, can an ethical life be consistent with the good life.

(Mandarin, London, 1994)

Quality of life: perspectives and policies

Sally Baldwin, Christine Godfrey and Carol Propper, eds

This collection of essays, predominantly by British writers, focuses on practical policy and methodology issues of measurement and service design for quality of life, giving special attention to problems of measuring the outcomes achieved by health and social care interventions. Given the roots of many of the writers in the York tradition in health economics, much space is devoted to the place, limits and controversial nature of the 'quality adjusted life year' measure in healthcare and analogous measures in the fields of disability. However, ethical challenges to the common and crude utilitarian uses of such measures are debated extensively. Although there has been much progress on technical matters in the decade since this work was done, this collection is still one of the best introductions to economic ideas of quality of life measurement in social policy.

(Routledge, London, 1991)

In pursuit of the quality of life

Avner Offer, ed

Offer's collection examines the quality of life in connection with the changing pattern of people's use of time, the impact of environmental quality, the quality of people's experience of work and conflicts between employment and child-rearing for the quality of parental life and relationships. It is less philosophical and more empirical than the Sen and Nussbaum collection but also addresses some of the arguments about capabilities, and is more wide-ranging than Baldwin *et al*. Offer's own contribution examines whether advertising is causing changes in expectations, degrading commitments to truth or diminishing the space for public life and trust, in ways that affect quality of life. A valuable and thought-provoking collection. If you only read one collection on quality of life, this is the one to choose.

(Oxford University Press, Oxford, 1996)

Book reviews compiled by Perri 6 and Emma Garman.

Recent publications from Demos

Civic entrepreneurship

Charles Leadbeater and Sue Goss
ISBN 1 898309 39 6 £9.95
The public sector is under increasing pressure to deliver improved services, while at the same time facing sweeping budget cuts. Yet it is slow to learn the lessons of good practice and to take on new roles. The authors argue that these problems can be overcome by encouraging entrepreneurship in the public sector to develop innovative solutions to local problems. Charles Leadbeater is a writer, journalist and Demos Research Associate. Sue Goss is Director of Local Services at the Office for Public Management.

The employee mutual: combining flexibility with security in the new world of work

Charles Leadbeater and Stephen Martin
ISBN 1 898309 94 9 £7.95
Today's labour market is more flexible and dynamic but also more insecure and uncertain. The authors propose a new labour market institution – the employee mutual – to help give people security and the ability to cope in this volatile work environment. The employee mutual would bring together workers and employers to find mutually beneficial solutions to shared problems, such as job search, training and childcare.

EuroVisions: new dimensions of European integration

Demos Collection issue 13
ISBN 1 898309 59 0
The European Union has focused on an institutional and economic agenda at the expense of strengthening its popular legitimacy and harnessing cultural forces for integration and common cause. This Collection lays out a new agenda for the EU based on the democratic, social and cultural dimensions of integration. Includes articles by Fritz W Scharpf, John Plender, Jon Browning and Ian Christie.

Learning beyond the classroom (Routledge)

Tom Bentley
ISBN 0 415 182 59 X £15.99
Education is a top priority for government but young people are having more difficulty than ever before in adapting to the world they will enter as adults. The author argues that we must recognise that learning takes place far beyond the formal education sector and connect what happens in schools to wider opportunities for learning.

Modernising the monarchy

Tim Hames and Mark Leonard
ISBN 1 898309 74 4 £4.95
After a controversial decade, the future of the monarchy has become the subject of considerable debate. The authors argue that the

monarchy must be modernised and restructured to concentrate exclusively on its symbolic functions, while down-grading its religious and political roles. They outline a programme for change that would allow the monarchy both to reflect public aspirations better and to find a mission appropriate to its place in a modern democracy.

On the right lines: the next centre-right in the British Isles

Perri 6
ISBN 1 898309 99 X £7.95
A provocative contribution to rethinking the basic philosophy of the centre-right. The author argues that Conservatism needs a new fusion between the ideas of neo-liberalism and Edmund Burke in order to tackle the challenges of globalisation, devolution and the future of the welfare state.

Rediscovering Europe

Mark Leonard
ISBN 1 898309 54 X £5.95
The European Union is less popular than it has been for a generation. It's core mission and institutions have become detached from the Europe found in people's everyday lives. The author offers a radical approach to legitimacy, using new data and analysis to highlight seven narratives which could reconnect the EU with the priorities and values of its citizens. Mark Leonard is a Senior Researcher at Demos.

Tomorrow's politics: the third way and beyond

Edited by Ian Hargreaves and Ian Christie
ISBN 1 898309 89 2 £7.95
This collections of essays aims to further the debate about the so-called 'third way' and the goals, policies and values the will be central to politics in the next century. Eleven essays on topics ranging from education to retirement set out possible ways forward in specific policy areas, and affirm that, now more than ever, we need progressive use of government.

Become a Demos subscriber

The price of annual subscription is £50.00 for individuals and £100.00 for institutions. *

You will receive:

● a minimum of four books (rrp £5.95–£14.95) containing policy, argument and analysis

● two issues of *Demos Collection* (rrp £8)

● one third off all Demos publications

● discounted entrance to Demos events

● any four existing publications free of charge (institutional subscriptions only)

* Subscribers outside Europe, please add £25.00 for airmail charges; subscribers in Australasia, please add £30.00.

Payment method direct debit / cheque
To pay by credit card, please ring Demos on 0171 353 4479.

Name

Address

Postcode

Telephone

DEM☉S

Originator number 626205

● DIRECT Debit

Instruction to your Bank or Building Society to pay Direct Debits

1 Name and full postal address of your Bank or Building Society

To The Manager

Bank or Building Society

Address

Postcode

2 Name(s) of account holder(s)

3 Branch sort code

(from top right hand corner of your cheque card)

☐☐ — ☐☐ — ☐☐

4 Bank or Building Society account number

☐☐☐☐☐☐☐☐

5 Demos reference number (for office use only)

6 Instruction to your Bank or Building Society:
Please pay Demos Direct Debits from the account detailed on this Instruction subject to the safeguards assured by the Direct Debit Guarantee.

Signature(s)

Date

Please send completed form to: Demos Freepost, London EC4B 4HP

Banks and building societies may not accept Direct Debit Instructions from certain types of account